MOVING PAST PTSD

For Tracy, my partner, my love . . .
and oh how we've laughed!

MOVING PAST PTSD

Consciousness, Understanding, and Appreciation for Military Veterans and Their Families

JAIME B. PARENT

Foreword by Danny K. Davis

ROWMAN & LITTLEFIELD
Lanham • Boulder • New York • London

Published by Rowman & Littlefield
An imprint of The Rowman & Littlefield Publishing Group, Inc.
4501 Forbes Boulevard, Suite 200, Lanham, Maryland 20706
www.rowman.com

6 Tinworth Street, London SE11 5AL, United Kingdom

British Library Cataloguing in Publication Information Available

Library of Congress Cataloging-in-Publication Data

Names: Parent, Jaime B., author.
Title: Moving past PTSD : consciousness, understanding, and appreciation for
    military veterans and their families / Jaime B. Parent.
Description: Lanham : Rowman & Littlefield, [2019] | Includes bibliographical
    references and index.
Identifiers: LCCN 2018057342 (print) | LCCN 2018057692 (ebook) | ISBN
    9781538127056 (electronic) | ISBN 9781538126967 (pbk. : alk. paper)
Subjects: | MESH: Combat Disorders | Stress Disorders, Post-Traumatic |
    Veterans Health | Veterans—psychology
Classification: LCC RC552.P67 (ebook) | LCC RC552.P67 (print) | NLM
    WM 184 | DDC 616.85/212—dc23
LC record available at https://lccn.loc.gov/2018057342

♾️™ The paper used in this publication meets the minimum requirements of
American National Standard for Information Sciences—Permanence of Paper for
Printed Library Materials, ANSI/NISO Z39.48-1992.

CONTENTS

Foreword by Danny K. Davis   vii

Prologue   ix

Acknowledgments   xvii

Part I: From Combat Stress to Invisible Wounds

1   Status Woe   3

2   Invisible Wounds   11

3   When War Games Get Real   15

4   When Innocence and the Innocents Die   25

5   A Gold Star Mom's PTSD   33

Part II: New Strategies for Transitioning Veterans

6   A Sense of Purpose   41

7   Careers, Not Jobs   51

8   At the Intersection of Human Spirit and Theology   61

9   Remembering Equality in the Workplace   67

10   New Clinical Therapies for New Types of War Injuries   75

11   You Cured My PTSD?   83

12   Not Your Father's VA   93

Part III: The Twenty-First-Century Veteran

13   Minority Report   101

14   The Transgender Veteran   111

15   Family Is a Circle of Strength   121

16   Being All In   131

17   I, Veteran   143

Epilogue: What You Can Do   149

Appendix: EN-Abled Veteran Internship Implementation Guide   157

Notes   167

Index   177

FOREWORD

It took 150 years, but five years ago, the National Museum of Civil War Medicine mounted its first exhibit on mental health, including displays on PTSD and suicide in the 1860s.

It is a gross understatement that we have been slow to recognize the impact of war on the human brain. The ensuing psychological damage resulting from war has had many names over the years: shell shock, combat fatigue, hysterical neurosis, posttraumatic stress disorder.

Doctors, military leaders, and elected officials confronted with addressing this trauma too often have faced conflicting interests in determining if their primary responsibility was to the warrior or the war effort. For far too long the interests of the warrior lost out and for far too long soldiers experiencing this trauma were stigmatized or ignored.

The history of veterans themselves taking leadership in demanding fulfillment of promises of heath care for returning veterans dates back to the Revolutionary War, the Civil War, and World War I. However, the war in Vietnam was a turning point for combat-related PTSD. Veterans advocated for themselves, demanding new understanding and real options for treatment and recovery.

Lieutenant Colonel, USAF (ret) Jaime B. Parent follows in that proud tradition. He has helped to re-frame combat-related PTSD as not only a medical issue, but as a *social* issue. He has not only been an advocate for veterans, he has been one of the movers and shakers in rethinking and re-creating organizations and gathering resources to treat returning veterans and their families as individuals each of whose return to civilian life confronts unique challenges.

The ultimate method of preventing combat-related PTSD is to stop war. It's long past time for us to understand and take that as a real and urgent mandate. In the meantime, *Moving Past PTSD: Consciousness, Understanding, and Appreciation for Military Veterans and Their Families* is a thought provoking, sometimes eye opening, always engrossing, intelligible, accessible glimpse into the world of the returning veteran and a practical guide into how each of us can help build a more welcoming and supportive society for our veterans and their families.

Danny K. Davis
Representative of the 7th Congressional District
of Illinois in the U.S. House of Representatives

PROLOGUE

The soldier above all others prays for peace, for it is the soldier who must suffer and bear the deepest wounds and scars of war.[1]

—General Douglas MacArthur

A rare combination of sun and wind was the order of the day. Wait a minute—this is Chicago, so this combination is not so rare, at least the wind anyway. Let's just say that spring was in the air as a fellow veteran named Pete and I made our way on Paulina Street in the Illinois Medical District on the west side of Chicago.

We were engaged in idle chatter during our short walk when all of a sudden I found myself walking alone, yet still talking. I turned around to find Pete stopped in his tracks on the sidewalk. "Hey," I shouted. "What's up?"

There was no response. Pete was still standing, a far gaze in his eyes. I thought to myself, "Well, we got some kind of deal going on here," which is the code phrase my wife, Tracy, and I use when we notice someone exhibiting different or unexpected behaviors. With a thirty-two-year-old son with autism at home and a great deal of experience with people with special needs, we have developed sharp instincts in recognizing behavioral differences.

It took me ten to fifteen seconds to walk back to where he was standing. I repeated my question, "Sooo, what's up?" Pete's voice was calm, but his face was pained.

He responded, "I can't walk down this street."

I asked him why and he pointed to what appeared to be an innocent looking Coke can on the pavement. "That thing is in front of me and I can't get any closer to it."

I thought for a moment. "OK, Pete, I get it. How about we just cross the street and then keep walking. Would that be OK?" He nodded and we proceeded without further incident or discussion as to why we had to cross the street. I saw Pete a couple of times after that incident, but we never spoke about what happened and why.

We didn't need to.

How would you have reacted in this situation? Confused? Afraid? Judgmental? Supportive? All of these would be understandable responses if you simply didn't know what was going on in Pete's head at the time. After all, this is not something you see every day nor are you prepared for what to do when it does happen.

To be honest, if I were not equipped with my acquired skill, attitude, experience, whatever you want to call it, that I learned from the disability community, I would probably have acted differently. I knew if I asked Pete a lot of questions or said something to the effect, "Oh, c'mon man. It's just a Coke can. You're back in the United States for crying out loud. Take it easy, will ya?" he would have felt worse about the situation and he may have acted differently. The last thing I wanted to do was put the onus on him to explain his reaction, which could make him feel that he was part of a problem. He wasn't, of course, but certainly I could have been.

When I got back to my office, I began to think about what was going on in the mind of this guy. I tried to rationalize and understand what he was thinking on that Chicago street and why he acted that way. I concluded that although I might not understand his reaction, I could still accept and support Pete's feelings and, with that understanding, could help Pete feel more at ease in a public setting.

But where do such feelings come from? Imagine you are a member of the U.S. military in a theater of operations far from home. By your side is an M-16 assault rifle. You sleep with it. You wake up with it each day, wondering how you're still alive. You fend off the enemy carrying a fifty-pound pack in 113 degree heat. You're wary of roadside bombs or snipers that can take you out or, worse, might kill your battle buddies right next to you. You depend upon these buddies and you share your food, your thoughts, and everything about your life with them. It's your job to keep them alive and their job to keep you alive.

Your enemy? They may be easily recognizable or may be someone with a machine gun behind a burka. You may have to climb into a truck at a moment's notice and not have any idea where you're going. You're always on edge. You get four hours a sleep a day and hardly any at night because that's the time for major operations. Your dehydrated meals ready to eat (MRE) have long passed their novelty, but they taste delicious anyway when you haven't eaten in twenty-four hours.

Suddenly, all of that is over and you're back home. You move to a new theater of operations: a reclining chair. By your side is a fifty-button TV remote. You sleep with it. You wake up every day wondering why you're still alive. You fend off enemies with the contents of a 750-ml bottle of vodka. You fear triggers and flashbacks or hurting your family. You fear yourself and what you will do. You get four hours of sleep a night and need alcohol to get there. You can't explain your feelings to anyone. They wouldn't understand anyway. Why bother? It's difficult to connect with loved ones who have no idea of your horrible past and current pain. They look on helplessly as they lose someone they once knew, and you know they're losing you. You long to go back overseas to that forward unit.

Many military soldiers, sailors, airmen, and marines returning home from combat are often emotionally and socially unrecognizable to the family and friends they left behind. The person that left for Iraq or Afghanistan may not be the same person who returns. In many instances, that person does not exist anymore. For that person, the flight home from the battlefield is just the beginning of a long and confusing journey.

Perhaps you have heard of or read stories about some of the challenges our returning veterans experience. You may have seen a news broadcast about a veteran who shot and killed people at work, school, or home. Maybe you have a veteran in your family, an older relative from Viet Nam, Korea, or even World War II. You may know a veteran who has served in Iraq and Afghanistan or someone who is still over there, still fighting.

The news and mainstream media are filled with different perspectives about our military and our veterans. Many books have been written on this subject from authors who have conducted extensive research or, perhaps, have been a veteran themselves. Often these books focus on a single purpose, such as finding a job, maximizing available benefits, or perhaps they want to share their personal story about life on the battlefield. Many heroes have written outstanding biographies that have offered comfort and inspiration to many readers.

One of the most compelling studies I have seen comes from researchers at Loyola University. In April 2016, the school published a comprehensive landmark study, "The State of the American Veteran: The Chicagoland Veteran Study." Chart 3-1 describes the challenges faced by the 240,000 and 360,000 veterans who leave the service every year, joining the 22 million veterans who have already served.

In 2013, Ken Simon, CEO of Walmart and president of U.S. operations, "announced that the retailing behemoth 'will offer a job to any honorably discharged veteran within his or her first twelve months off active duty.' The company expects the number of hires to reach 100,000."[2]

I wondered whether or not just "any jobs" were a good fit for veterans. Not going into specifics or judgment here, but were minimum wage jobs something that military veterans would want? I'm sure the answer for some is yes, but many veterans expressed to me that they wanted more than just a job; they wanted a second career. They wanted to continue to serve but didn't know how to get there. Could we do better at providing skilled civilian jobs for those veterans that wanted them?

Having had a successful career in healthcare information technology (HIT) post military, I thought about whether there might be opportunities for veterans in healthcare. Healthcare careers are in demand, as well as general information technology (IT) careers in many different types of businesses. What if we could put the two together to provide career opportunities for veterans?

Thus, the EN-Abled Veteran Internship focuses on HIT and general IT. I researched and conducted interviews to determine what veterans need, how quickly those needs could be met, and what innovative methods could be developed. I discovered that while school and training opportunities were helpful, some veterans needed help immediately. Some were having cars repossessed and homes taken away because they had no job. They couldn't wait two years to get a degree. They needed job help right away and building a quick and effective internship was the answer.

At its core, the EN-Abled Veteran Internship is a thirteen-week on-the-job internship that provides individual training for veterans preparing for a job (or career) in IT. It is unique in nature and form. No job is promised, as the design is to have the internship reproducible anywhere, regardless of industry or location. But if jobs were available at a particular company, then the veteran intern could get permanent placement, but only if he or she competed fairly with nonveterans of similar skill and experience. No one wanted charity, especially, veterans.

I created the EN-Abled Veteran website[3] with all the information needed for organizations to build, market, and grow their own EN-Abled Veteran Internship. Partnering with business, government, and technology firms, close to fifty veterans in fifteen states have begun IT careers. Epic systems, a leading provider of electronic medical records, has partnered with the EN-Abled Veteran Internship and to date, thirty veterans have achieved different Epic certifications since 2014.[4] The reach of the EN-Abled Veteran Internship spans eighteen organizations offering multiple entry level IT job placements in Chicago, both in and out of healthcare.

While the EN-Abled Veteran Internship was beginning to gain momentum, across the street from Rush University Medical Center another veterans program was getting under way. The Road Home Program was being established as a separate not-for-profit activity that would focus on specific needs for veterans and their families facing such complex issues as traumatic brain injury (TBI), posttraumatic stress disorder (PTSD), and military sexual trauma (MST). Road Home was not meant to supplant any or all activities of the Veterans Administration. Rather, Road Home's mission is to compassionately serve veterans and their families, providing individualized care and navigation of services to help heal the invisible wounds of war.[5]

As a member of the Wounded Warrior Network, the Road Home Program has grown in both size and scope. Through a $45 million matching grant, the Road Home Program brings comprehensive complex care, counselling, and the latest in diagnostics and therapies to returning veterans. Other programs through the Robert R. McCormick Foundation and Boeing have resulted in strong community support and a new bedrock for veterans services throughout the Midwest.

I became excited as I started to see the success of both EN-Abled Veteran Internship and Road Home Program each with independent missions but common goals. While the Road Home Program focused on clinical support, social programs, and family treatments, EN-Abled Veteran was achieving equal success with vocational training and job placement— supported by the incredible leadership and nurturing environment that is Rush University Medical Center. It would be a great partnership at a great academic medical center.

As the programs began to grow and mature, I began speaking with support staff, veterans, and their families. I gained incredible insight and gathered many stories as to what is happening with veterans today. A world of trust was built at Rush University Medical Center across a wide spectrum of the human condition. Incredible stories of strength, perseverance, love, and respect mushroomed in the lives of everyone who came in contact with a veteran. The organization changed in so many ways, quickly and passionately; something I never could have predicted but was so blessed to witness.

I decided to start documenting these stories and learn as much as I could about this transformation. As I dug deeper, veterans, family members, clinicians, and coworkers opened up to me in a way I never imagined.

Often I would interview someone and they would say, "You should talk to so-and-so," or "Have you thought about this?" And so the web of love and understanding simply grew larger and more encompassing.

The interviews gave me insight into some very sensitive subjects, often taboo in mainstream media: racism, sexual harassment, prejudice, frustration, and overwhelming heartbreak at multiple levels. There was no holding back. The stories are real and are told here for the first time. Many veterans gave full permission to use their first and last names in the narrative. If the veteran was not available for this verification, pseudonyms and first names were used.

Today, we have innovative treatments and advances in technology and transportation to effectively treat battlefield injuries and save lives. Advanced triage and transport get the wounded quickly to field hospitals. Military personnel who would have bled to death on the battlefield now survive their injuries. Advances in prosthetics greatly enhance the quality of life for those injured by roadside bombs.

Legislatively, the U.S. government has introduced new programs and funding that provide for scholarships and low interest loans and mortgages to help veterans get benefits and find a home. Hundreds of for-profit and not-for-profit organizations, many of them established by fellow veterans, reach out to veterans and their families every day offering a wide range of services. Educational grants have given veterans the opportunity to get a college degree or learn a trade. The Veterans Administration (VA) Health System is funded at its highest level in history.

But we as a society still seem to miss the mark and have yet to find the balance that provides for all veterans. While the unemployment rate for veterans has levelled off to equal that of nonveteran counterparts,[6] underemployment affects more veteran job seekers than nonveteran applicants. Nearly one-third of veteran job seekers are underemployed—a rate 15.6 percent higher than nonveteran job seekers. Sometimes this is due to a mismatch between their military skills and experience and the civilian labor market.[7]

VA hospitals and clinics cannot treat the sheer volume of veterans who come to them with complex physical and psychological needs. Our colleges and vocational schools, and the processes needed to gain admission, cannot keep up with the number of veterans using their benefits to take classes or get degrees. Many times veterans find themselves lost, without purpose, unmotivated, and trapped in what they perceive to be a gyre of broken promises, misinformation, and betrayal. Perhaps the most loathsome statistic of all is the fact that we lose a veteran to suicide every sixty-five minutes.[8] Some believe this number is much higher.

Also complicating life for veterans are the stigmas associated with being in the military. Perhaps you have heard some of them.

- Ex-military are too rigid and inflexible.
- A lot of them have PTSD and are dangerous to be around.
- Veterans are physically abusive and sexually aggressive and violent.
- Veterans are so messed up that they can't adjust to a civilian work environment.
- All veterans are looking for is a handout.

As for veterans, they two have their own set of institutional biases:

- No one will hire me.
- I served four years protecting my country. I deserve a job.
- I'm fine; nothing to see here.
- I'm not that sick. Let someone else who needs the appointment take that slot.
- No one understands what I've been through.
- Everything is an empty promise.
- I don't think they really want to hire veterans anyway.

Sadly, these points are direct quotes from conversations I have had with veterans and nonveterans. Hard to believe? Well, think about these questions. "Should I put my military experience on a resume? What if I have a disability? Should I identify myself as someone who is disabled?" A job application is where the misconceptions of veterans and nonveterans intersect. I've struggled with the answers to these questions myself. What would you do?

Some veterans embrace readjustment and go on with successful lives. Some veterans merely pretend to cope better than others. Many struggle, and it's really hard sometimes to tell one from another. The power of pride varies. The thought of seeking help stings some but not others. A veteran told me that he did not want to seek medical treatment because he felt that he was taking away an appointment from someone who "needs to see a doctor more than I do."

One thing is certain: there are veterans all around you, at work, in your neighborhood, your school, or your place of worship. You'll also find veterans from all walks of life in all career fields. Curiously, some veterans gravitate toward politics. As a result of the 2018 midterm elections, the total number of lawmakers with military experience for the 116th Congress is ninety-six, but that is six less than the start of the last congressional session. The number of lawmakers with military experience has been in a steady decline since the Viet Nam War when 75 percent of members in Congress had military experience, a normal attrition due to the numbers who served in World War II versus the numbers who have served since Viet Nam. Next year's Congress will boast the largest number of female veterans in history (six) and the largest class of freshmen veteran lawmakers in a decade (nineteen).[9]

Some veterans have built their own businesses and continue their service in their communities. Some become teachers, policemen, or firemen. But on the other darker side, many veterans suffer in silence. A 2016 study found that there are 39,471 veterans still homeless on the streets of America.[10]

Being a retired U.S. Air Force lieutenant colonel, I thought I knew a lot about veterans. But as I conducted more and more interviews, I was humbled by just how much I didn't know about what is really going on behind the headlines. What was once simply a primer focusing on vocational opportunity became more expansive and exhaustive as I found a vista of what is really going on with our veterans.

I learned a lot about veterans' conditions, something I thought I knew but discovered that I was not as enlightened as I thought. I experienced a wave of emotion that I didn't anticipate. Overwhelmed by the heartache, strength, resolve, and determination of both veterans and support staff, I often went home and simply closed the door to my bedroom, overwhelmed by the pain, suffering, and the impetuous passion that overcame me on a daily basis.

After life in the military, moving to life *after* the military presents monumental challenges for everyone involved. There is a common thread; the military member has changed, but so has the family. Both sides, who have grown apart, are forced to come together after spending significant time in different worlds. Coming home for the veteran means different things to different veterans. It's more than parades, clean sheets, fast food, and football. It's more than hanging up "Welcome Home" banners and tying ribbons on trees. It's a complex ecosystem of medical and emotional needs, expectations, apprehensions, and, in some cases, more terror than the world left behind.

In this book you will learn not only how to identify issues but constructive ways you can help and how you can contribute and improve the quality of life for our returning military veterans. You will see and understand the complete life cycle of the warfighter coming home and what this means to all types of veterans, families, clinicians, friends, and coworkers. Such a comprehensive yet personal story has never been written.

Until now.

ACKNOWLEDGMENTS

The author would like to acknowledge the following for their help with this book:

From the Road Home Program: Mark Pollack, MD, Niranjan Karnik, MD, PhD, Michael Brennan, MD, Chris Miller, Will Beiersdorf, Tanya Friese, DNP, RN, CNL, Tanjilisa Williams, and Gold Star Mom Modie Lavin

From Rush University Medical Center: Lac Tran and Bobby Clapp

From the Department of Veterans Affairs, North Chicago, IL: Demetrice Barnes

From the Office of the 7th Congressional District (IL), the Honorable Congressman Danny K. Davis, Assistants Josie Ware and Ira Cohen

From Epic Systems: CEO Judy Faulkner, Liz Sugden and Katie O'Brien

From the Information Technology industry leaders supporting the EN-Abled Veteran internship training: Cisco, Citrix, Dell, EMC2, Epic Systems, Hewlett Packard, Hitachi Data Systems, Lexmark, Microsoft, NetApp, Trend Micro, and VMware

From the staff at the Rush University Medical Center Information Technology Department: Kimberly Jackson, Dwaine Goings, Abdelkrim Belkhos, Marlene Bailey, Tommy Bankhead, Trevor Stone, Terri Ibanez, Juan Duran, Ahmad Hasan, Debra Ingram, and honorary veteran Andy Bowe

For perspectives on spousal support for veterans: Janet Vasquez

From the LGBTQ veteran community: Rabbah Rona Matlow, Rebecca Solen

From the CAPTAIN James A. Lovell Federal Health Care Center Department of Psychiatry: Corinne Belsky, MD

From Cone Health System: Robert Smith (EN-Abled Veteran template)

From CBS2 Chicago: Anchorman Rob Johnson

From WCPT860 radio: "Thank you for your service" program with Antonio Correa

From Abbe Lyle Photography: Abbe Lyle

From the Blackberry Café: The Reverend Lon Thompson, James Martin, CMD, USN, (retired), Frank Bunn, CMD, USN (retired) and Sherry Lipe

From the WNBA: The Chicago Sky

From Rowman and Littlefield: Editors Christine Fahey and Kathryn Knigge

From Brookes Publishing: Proposal editor Liz Gildea

And most importantly, these successful interns from the from the EN-Abled Veteran Internship, some of whom have been working in the technology related field for over 4 years: Sean D'Sauveterre, Keith Garcia, Keith Gonzalez, Andre Hall, Andre Hampton, Bogumila Kenny, Joseph Kline, Richard Manu, Ken Marion, Willie Mayers, Matthew McCoy, Peter Meyer, Liz Michalski, Darueshi (Dart) Moseberry, Robert Neal III, Olatunbosun (Tobi) Olatunji, Ryan Russell, Sid Stein, Cassandra Taylor, Mark Truitt, Ivan Vasquez, and James Wigfall.

I

FROM COMBAT STRESS TO INVISIBLE WOUNDS

1

STATUS WOE

History repeats itself, but in such cunning disguise that we never detect the resemblance until the damage is done.[1]

—Sydney J. Harris, American journalist

Fred and Al are two Army guys returning home from World War II. This conversation is from the opening scenes of the movie *The Best Years of Our Lives*, which resonated so well with post–World War II moviegoers that it took home nine Oscars, including Best Picture of 1946. Captain Fred Deery and Platoon Sergeant Al Stephenson have this conversation while flying in a small plane across the United States as they head home:

Fred: Hey, Al.

Al: Yeah?

Fred: Remember what it felt like when you went overseas?

Al: As well as I remember my own name.

Fred: I feel the same way now. Only more so.

Al: I know what you mean.

Fred: Just nervous out of the service, I guess. The thing that scares me most is that everybody's gonna try to rehabilitate me. All I want's a good job, a mild future, and a house big enough for me and my wife. Give me that much and I'm rehabilitated like that [snaps his fingers].

Al: I'd say that's not too much to ask.[2]

Six decades later, today's veterans want the same thing.

From a civilian point of view, leaving the United States to go off to a foreign land is a dramatic leap into the unknown. But in reality, it isn't. Military personnel go through extensive training, physically and psychologically, so that by the time they are deployed, they are well prepared for their new environment. The emotional and mental changes start in training, not on the battlefield.

There is no such training for preparing the warfighter coming back home. Like Fred and Al, many get dropped back home with little or no transitional training except for taking a class or attending a couple of briefings. Physically, they find themselves back in their hometown, in a routine they were once familiar with but now can no longer process. Home is now foreign, the battlefield is familiar, and there is not enough preparation for this new normal. Mentally, many veterans are still back in the war zone, an environment they were trained to learn about and respect because death could come at any moment. Back home, they are safe in their beds, until the nightmares of the past resurface in horrific dreams about what went down.

Some veterans I interviewed can't sleep in a bed anymore. Instead, they sleep on the floor or, if possible, under a bed—a place of solace and protection. Trying to explain this to a spouse or significant other can be difficult or impossible, especially if the veteran is not open to talking about battlefield experiences.

Bad habits and destructive behaviors begin to set in. This is especially true for those veterans who self-medicate. One veteran told me that the "happy hour" started at 5 p.m., got moved to 2 p.m., and then got moved to waiting in the parking lot for the liquor store to open at 9 a.m.

Author of the acclaimed book *WWII*, James Jones describes these coming-home-from-war experiences not as readjustment or transition but as the "de-evolution" of the soldier.

Yet just as with earlier wars, America struggles with how to deal with those coming home. While they flashed back to horrific events related to fellow soldiers and perhaps little children, their husbands or wives sat straight up in bed in their new nightwear bought especially for the homecoming, wide-eyed and staring, horrified.

Slowly, bit by bit, it began to taper off. But men still woke up in the middle of the night, thrashing around and trying to get their hands on their wives' throats. Men still rolled out of bed in a dead sleep and hit the floor with a crash, huddling against the bed. In terms of the lack of infrastructure support for transitioning military veterans, lessons learned from World War II have been learned but not applied.[3]

Help is available, yet it is inconsistent and often inadequate. Limited access to healthcare and lack of benefits counselling and vocational training leaves many of our veterans with untreated healthcare issues and few job prospects. Many wander aimlessly, lingering at the VA, living on the street or in homeless shelters, or, worse, committing suicide.

Some have too much pride to seek help.

Veteran benefits align with the specific time of service during a specific period of war. A pre-9/11 veteran has different benefit opportunities than a Desert Storm veteran who has different benefits as an Iraq veteran, who has different benefits than a Viet Nam veteran.

In addition to specific healthcare eligibility, there are different types of GI Montgomery bills for different types of educational opportunities. Active duty, reservists, pre- and post-9/11 veterans get a variety of benefits and entitlements. Medical care is available, free of charge from the VA, but it may take weeks or months to get an appointment. Often, disability claim benefits can take months, even years, to resolve. Recently, the VA experienced problems with reimbursing veterans. Because of computer "IT problems," many veterans haven't received GI Bill benefits for months due to ongoing IT issues at the VA. "Department of Veterans Affairs Secretary Robert Wilkie overruled a top benefits official and said the VA won't ignore federal law and will now reimburse veterans who may have been underpaid GI Bill benefits."[4]

Helpful, but not timely and nothing new. These types of transitional missteps for veterans are not new; they have been occurring since World War I.

"When veterans of World War I returned home in the early 1920s, they petitioned Congress to offer some sort of compensation for lost wages; military pay was far below what they could have earned at home in the factories," writes author Brandon Weber. "Congress passed a law to compensate them, but the certificates issued to the veterans were not payable until 1945. Meanwhile, in 1932, the Great Depression was in full swing, and those veterans became part of the destitute masses who had no money, no food, no jobs, and, in some cases, no homes."[5]

Little progress was made between the two World Wars. Michael D. Gambone, professor of history at Kutztown University, offers this perspective of returning veterans:

> For the GI generation, accommodation became an increasingly prevalent expectation. On one level, many of these changes were definitely for the good. The utility of military service to advance the cause of civil

rights was a breakthrough in the forties that energized minorities in America and led inexorably to further pressure for reform in the fifties and sixties. Similarly, the scramble set off by college and universities intent on capturing federal dollars, coupled with the demands made by veterans for entry into higher education, ended an atmosphere of exclusivity that had prevented many aspiring students from advancing their education. . . .

Unfortunately, access came at the cost of rising student-faculty ratios, stadium seating in introductory courses, vast dorm complexes that clustered students together in unheard-of numbers, and a growing depersonalization of learning.[6]

America sways back and forth in its response to warfighters returning home, especially when Viet Nam is included. Much of this is based on the political climate. Only when the United States was attacked at Pearl Harbor did the "How dare they" patriotic response kick in. The Army and Navy saved the world and returning veterans were showered with love and ticker tape parades. But the lack of transitioning support remained. Ken Moffett, in his essay "Coming Home," adds further comments on the returning of veterans narrative:

Traditionally, America has always supported its armed forces and has shown great respect for those in uniform. In 1919, at the end of World War I, the Doughboys returned home from Europe to ticker-tape victory parades, marching bands, speeches, and the good will of all Americans. Additionally, when the soldiers returned home from World War II and the Korean War, they were treated as heroes. A euphoric atmosphere overtook the nation, and celebrations were held in their honor all around the country. Unfurled American flags that decorated streets and homes could be seen waving in the breeze. It was as if they, too, were welcoming home the G.I.'s. The reveling continued non-stop for weeks; it seemed as though the nation and its citizens could not do enough for the returning service men and women. A grateful nation was anxious to show its admiration and support to the returning soldiers.

Unfortunately, this was not the case when the soldiers returned home from Vietnam. As a result of America's loss in Vietnam, there was a misperception that the men who fought there did not measure up to their predecessors in World War II and Korea. "Nothing could be further from the truth," said General Frederick C. Weyand, United States Army. During the course of General Weyand's military career, he served in World War II, Korea, and Vietnam. While in Vietnam, General Weyand commanded the Twenty-fifth Infantry Division, the division portrayed in the film Platoon. General Weyand estimates that during his tours, he visited soldiers in the field more than one thousand times. And, despite the negative and hostile attitude of the news media—not only towards the war but also towards the soldiers—the morale and spirits of the soldiers remained high.

Perhaps the cruelest aspect of the war was the treatment of the returning soldiers. Unlike the hero status given to the returning soldiers form World War II, the soldiers that served in Vietnam were portrayed as baby killers, psychos, drug addicts and war mongers. It was not an uncommon scene for returning soldiers to be confronted at airports by protesters carrying signs with anti-war slogans. The protesters used the signs to attack the soldiers and even threw urine at the veterans. In some instances, soldiers were refused service in restaurants. I remember an incident after I returned home; one of my close friends and I were walking down a street in Oakland, California, when a filthy, long-haired, flea-infested piece of street trash approached us and began yelling insults at us. Mike wanted to take him out right there, but we decided to pass it up. This common sight on the streets of America during the Vietnam War years was in no way reminiscent of the homecoming given the returning soldiers from previous wars.[7]

Historically, the United States has been hesitant to go to war. Congress has not declared war since 1942, when war was declared on Germany, Italy, Romania, Hungary, and Bulgaria.[8] War against Korea and Viet Nam, and the current "war on terror," were never declared wars. Today, military conflicts have been curiously relabeled as "operations" (Desert Shield, Desert Storm, Enduring Freedom, Iraqi Freedom). Authority is now referred to as "authorization for use of force," and emanates from a presidential executive order.

In short, the president can send troops in and pull troops out without congressional oversight or approval. And he has been doing so since World War II.

The result is an escalation in the number of armed conflicts. Approximately 150 countries (37 European) have U.S. military personnel living and/or working within them, according to the U.S. Department of Defense. As of March 31, 2008, there are 433,120 personnel deployed outside the fifty states; March 27, 2009 had that number listed as just over 500,000.[9] U.S. Senators expressed surprise when in late 2017 four Green Berets were killed in an ambush in Niger. Many didn't even know we had soldiers in that part of the world. As of this writing, eighteen years after 9/11, the United States is still mired in prolonged and deeply complicated military operations without a clear exit strategy or winning formula.

"What we've learned is that you can't really leave," said a senior Pentagon official with extensive experience in Afghanistan and Iraq who, like others, spoke on the condition of anonymity to describe internal discussions. "The local forces need air support, intelligence, and help with logistics. They are not going to be ready in three years or five years. You have to be there for a very long time."[10]

Unlike previous wars, there is no clear enemy, no clear organizational or territorial geography to go after. There is no country to defeat, no one ideology to overcome. Estimates are that close to 105,000 Japanese citizens were killed during the nuclear bombings of Hiroshima and Nagasaki.[11] Today there is a concerted effort to limit civilian casualties, making wars more difficult to fight. No longer can the United States rely upon its massive military strength to gain advantage in wartime situations. The air power advantage and military might of the United States for these new types of wars is handcuffed. Suicide bombers from numerous terrorist cells infiltrate democracies and bring war to our own American streets, schools, and doorsteps. These types of terrorist attacks surprised America and we are still grappling with strategies to deal with these new types of threats. Don't be misled. These are not just threats from the so-called radical Islamic state. Hate groups with unbelievable and inexplicable evil in their hearts are promoting violence and it is being conducted by American citizens, on our own soil, not some faraway land. Members of the House of Representatives are being gunned down during baseball practice. Children and teachers are being murdered in their own classrooms. Nazi marches are held at American universities. The horrors of war and the shedding of innocent blood are causing PTSD in citizens who wear no military uniform. Social media and cable TV bring all of these graphics into our homes 24/7, sometimes with the same images streaming over and over again. This enemy has no borders. This enemy has no conscience. It roams freely from country to country, wherever soft targets exist. America is fighting this enemy, but at the same time, we are fighting ourselves—internal terrorists, men and women who blow up churches, schools, and movie theaters. Oftentimes, wars are fought with fuzzy borders. On any given day, it's a blur as to who or what the United States is really fighting, ISIS or its own people.

There appears to be no shortage of men, women, or children who will detonate a bomb taped to their chest, taking out themselves and dozens of others. There are few things people will die for. Many used to die for freedom. Today, many die for a religious belief, martyrdom, or both. All of these things contribute to the potential for PTSD.

Retired army colonel Charles W. Hoge, MD, comments in his book *Once a Warrior, Always a Warrior* on what he refers to as contradictions of PTSD:

> PTSD is full of contradictions. Virtually every reaction that mental health professionals label a "symptom," and which indeed can cause havoc in your life after returning home from combat, is an essential survival skill in the war zone. The dilemma is that the reactions that are necessary for survival and success in combat are not easy to dial down and adapt after coming home. Society believes that a warrior should be able to transition home and lead a "normal" life, but the reality is that most of society has no clue what it means to be a warrior.[12]

Today's wars are fought in both foreign and domestic battlefields. Terms like *cyberwar, jihad,* and *surgical strikes* are commonly used in modern warfare. Medical treatment and triage have also gone through modernization. In previous wars, losing a limb, sustaining a head injury, or other serious wounds resulted in death right there on the battlefield. With modern and sophisticated triage methods and advances in medicine, aviation, and technology, lives that would have been lost are now being saved.

There are about 18 million veterans in the United States; almost half of them are age sixty-five or older. Approximately 1.5 million are women and 135,000 are transgender. Close to 78 percent are white, 12 percent black, and 6 percent Hispanic. Predictably, California, Florida, and Texas have the highest number of veterans (3 million). Approximately 28 percent have a college degree and the median income is $34,000 per year. There are 7.2 million veterans in the labor force with 400,000 of them unemployed. Four million have a service connected disability.[13]

Yes, today's wars are different and so are the casualties. We have created a generation of Americans with silent torment, injuries that cannot be seen with the naked eye nor treated in conventional ways. We have created a generation with invisible wounds.

2

INVISIBLE WOUNDS

Unexpressed emotions will never die. They are buried alive and will come forth later in uglier ways.[1]

—Sigmund Freud

Astronaut Chris Hadfield is a Canadian astronaut who spent 144 days on the International Space Station. He is a true hero known for his great courage and emotional strength, along with a pretty good guitar rendition of David Bowie's hit "Space Oddity." An engaging speaker and educator, Chris travelled over 61 million miles completing 2,336 orbits of Earth.

Along with fellow astronauts Tom Marshburn of NASA and Russian Roman Romanenko, he landed in Kazakhstan following a 146-day mission to the International Space Station. Chris has shared his experiences as to what coming home from space was like. Here is a summation of his remarks as keynote speaker for Trend Micro's "Directions '17" annual conference.

After all that time in zero gravity, I felt like an old man. My blood pressure was off and I could only stand for a very short period of time. My body was quite happy in space. But now, my body couldn't support my head. I could barely stand, let alone walk.

They put me in special clothing because I couldn't keep my blood pressure within normal limits. My body was not used to supporting my head so my neck, spine, and back were in constant pain. I tried to talk but my tongue was so heavy, all I did was babble and drool. And when the capsule hit the earth, I felt as if I were in a terrible car crash. Even my eyelids required heavy lifting.

There's a YouTube video out there which documents our return to earth. There were people and cameras all over the place and the last thing I wanted was to have my picture taken. People wanted to try to talk to me and all I had was this weird smile on my face.

I knew I had to do something, so the only thing I could muster was a thumb's up sign. The truth is, I was in agony. I wanted everyone to go away because all I wanted to do was turn my head to the side and throw up.[2]

As I listened to Chris, all I could think of were the experiences of some military veterans returning from the battlefield. For these returning heroes, the return home was also some type of alien experience. Chris Hadfield's mind and body changed in space. The military mind and body changed in Afghanistan. Granted, Chris Hadfield has some serious physiological problems going from zero to Earth's gravity. He spent several months in serious rehabilitation as his body required major occupational and physical therapy.

And, by the way, just like a military veteran who feels more comfortable on the battlefield, if there's a one-way mission to Mars coming up, Chris Hadfield wants to be on it.

Historically, *shell shock*, *battle fatigue*, the *thousand-mile stare* are among the terms used to describe mentally impaired veterans coming home. Today, with a greater understanding of the pathology and treatment for the mentally ill, these terms have been replaced by *TBI*, *PTSD*, and a broader term, *invisible wounds*.

During World War I, it became clear that injuries that affected the psyche of the soldier needed to be separated and treated differently. The number of casualties from the Great War were staggering. Questions arose as to whether mental illness was related directly to the experience of war or perhaps more dependent upon the character, courage, toughness, and so on, of patients experiencing service-related traumatic experiences.

The British Army was particularly alarmed by the growing number of servicemen returning from war who were suffering some type of unspecified aberrant behavior.

By the end of World War, I, the [British] army had been forced to deal with 80,000 cases of "shell shock," a term first used in 1917 by a medical officer named Charles Myers to describe the physical damage done to soldiers on the front lines during exposure to heavy bombardment.

It soon became clear, however, that the various symptoms of shell shock—including debilitating anxiety, persistent nightmares, and physical afflictions ranging from diarrhea to loss of sight—were appearing even in soldiers who had never been directly under bombardment, and the meaning of the term was broadened to include not only the physical but the psychological effects produced by the experience of combat.[3]

While Dr. Charles Myers believed that he could treat individual patients, the greater problem was how to manage the mass volumes that returned home following major military offensives. Drawing on ideas developed by French military neuropsychiatrists, Myers identified three essentials in the treatment of shell shock: "promptness of action, suitable environment and psychotherapeutic measures," though those measures were often limited to encouragement and reassurance.[4]

Myers argued that the military should set up specialist units "as remote from the sounds of warfare as is compatible with the preservation of the 'atmosphere' of the front."[5] The army took his advice and allowed him to set up four specialist units in December 1916. They were designed to manage acute or mild cases, while chronic and severe cases were referred to base hospitals for more intensive therapy.

During 1917, the battles of Arras, Messines, and Passchendaele produced a flood of shell-shock cases, overwhelming the four units. Inevitably, Myers was criticized by those who believed that shell shock was simply cowardice or malingering. Some thought the condition would be better addressed by military discipline.

Nevertheless, the principles of forward psychiatry that Myers identified—prompt treatment as close to the fighting as is safe, with an expectation of recovery and return to unit—were widely adopted during World War II by both the U.S. and U.K. military, and they continue to be practiced by Western armed forces today in Afghanistan and Iraq.[6]

The *Diagnostic and Statistical Manual of Mental Disorders* published by the American Psychiatric Association provides a common language and set of standard criteria for the classification of mental illness and syndromes. It is used by a wide range of disciplines, including doctors, researchers, drug companies, health insurers, pharmaceutical companies, legal and government organizations.

Beyond a set of standards and the advances in practice and diagnosis tools over the last one hundred years, what have we learned about the experiences of the warfighter in previous wars? One thing we've learned: veterans' PTSD claims have tripled in the last decade.[7]

Stephen Joseph, PhD, is a professor of psychology, health, and social care at the University of Nottingham, and author of *What Doesn't Kill Us*:

> Is shell shock the same as PTSD? This is an intriguing question. I believe that PTSD and shell shock are the same, yet they are different. The same because shell shock was an intellectual forerunner to PTSD. PTSD was influenced by the experiences of psychiatrists working with veterans returning from Vietnam. As such the two ideas set out to do the same thing.[8]

Erin P. Finley is a medical anthropologist and investigator at the Veterans Evidence-Based Research Dissemination and Implementation Center (VERDICT), Department of Veterans Affairs Medical Center, San Antonio, Texas. Her widely referenced book *Fields of Combat* examines PTSD as it relates to two major focal points—personal experience and cultural politics. According to Finley,

> [C]ombat trauma is only one of many kinds of experiences that cumulatively increase the risk of developing PTSD. Post-deployment knocks such as the inability to reintegrate into family and community life, divorce, unemployment, and so forth play an important role in exacerbating PTSD risk among recent veterans.
>
> When veterans return from war to find that what they thought would be a chance to create new post-combat lives is, in fact, far more challenging than they ever imagined—when they find themselves dislocated for their loved ones and struggling to meet their most basic expectations for self and life—these challenges make it far more difficult to muster a resilient response to the trauma of war.[9]

Astronaut Chris Hadfield's return home was a huge change from the environment he had become accustomed to. Much is the same for our military veterans upon returning from the environment they have been accustomed to.

3

WHEN WAR GAMES GET REAL

He drew a circle that shut me out—Heretic, rebel, a thing to flout. But love and I had the wit to win: We drew a circle and took him In![1]

—Edwin Markham, poet

The twenty-year period following the Viet Nam War saw the United States involved in skirmishes with other countries that involved minimal resources and lasted days in duration. With the reunification of Germany and the economic collapse of the Soviet Union, the United States stood alone as the world's superpower. Such status began to evolve to something more of a world's policeman, with relatively easy victories in Somalia, Panama, Libya, and Grenada. A complacency began to creep in because the United States could use its mighty forces to move in quickly with minimal effort, accomplish the mission, and move on.

This was the case when Iraq invaded Kuwait.

In preparing for a war against Iraq, military planners seem to anticipate a walkover. The Iraqi military performed badly in the Gulf War of 1991: Saddam Hussein promised the mother of all battles, but his troops delivered instead the mother of all bugouts. And the planners note that Iraq is even weaker now.

Moreover, the regime appears to enjoy very little support. Saddam Hussein lives in such fear of his own military forces that he keeps them out of Baghdad. It is generally anticipated that most of the military will not fight for him—indeed, that there may be substantial defections to the invaders even among the comparatively coddled Republican Guard.

In addition, the regime really controls only a share of the country. The Kurds have established a semi-independent entity in the north, and the hostility toward Saddam's rule is so great in the Shiite south that government officials often consider the region hostile territory.[2]

Such was the culture Marine Corporal Chris Miller entered in early 2003.

"My name is Chris Miller, I am the senior outreach coordinator for the Road Home Program in Chicago. I served in the Marines from 2000 to 2004. I was a 'toe gunner' in the infantry. My platoon was called a mixture of machine guns, javelins, explosive and the toe missile systems mounted on trucks.

"I went to a faith based high school and upon graduation attended the University of Louisville where I was totally not ready for college. Louisville wasn't an all boy's school, it was not strict, and it was a lot of fun. I had tons of freedom—let's use it. So I was successful in partying my way out of two semesters. I took some odd jobs, had my own apartment, but when the business I was working at went bankrupt, I started heading down a bad path and was starting to get into trouble.

"Growing up, I always knew in the back of my head in high school that the military was always an option. One day, I visited an Army recruiter, even though I had no real knowledge of the military except for *Full Metal Jacket* and *Rambo* movies in the late 1990s. I did extremely well on the Army skills examination, but they wanted to put me in intelligence and a college track. I left that office and walked right next door to the Marine recruiter who had a really cool poster of a guy coming out of the swamp, wearing grease paint and carrying a rifle. I saw that picture and I immediately said, 'Sign me up for that. That really looks like fun.' And it was.

"I wanted to play GI Joe for four years, so driving trucks and blowing stuff up sounded great. Five days later after leaving the Marine recruiter's office, I was in Paris Island assigned to the 3rd battalion, 1st Marine Division at Camp Pendleton. Our first deployment was five months to Okinawa, Japan, where we trained and travelled all over Southeast Asia. We had fun, came back home, and were about to do it all over again.

"Then 9/11 hit. Training got real that day. From that day forward, it was a completely different atmosphere. I thought I was going to enjoy four years of surfing in Southern California and a couple of tours to Thailand and Southeast Asia. I got to see [life] before 9/11 as a Marine, but I was not prepared for what was ahead of me.

"We started working immediately. In February of 2003, after several days of beer and keg parties on the beach, we got a phone call to get our gear together in four hours. I made a few phone calls to my grandma. I got meritoriously promoted in the parking lot at Pendleton to the rank of corporal. OK, now time to get on the bus. With huge hangovers [*laughs*], we drove to March Air Force Base. We immediately got on a plane where after refueling in the air over New York, we landed in Marón, Spain.

"We were supposed to immediately refuel and go to Kuwait, but the plane broke down and we were stuck in Marón for three to four days while we waited for parts to come in. Needless to say, we had beer, wild parties, and bar scenes just like you see in the old west films, where bottles are everywhere and chairs and fists were flying. Several Marines got arrested and spent the night in a Spanish prison. It was not good, especially when the European Command got involved. It was kind of a shit show of the night. Lots of trouble was to follow.

"We had outstanding leadership and we were a very senior group of Marines. My regimental commander was Joe Dunford who later was named Chairman of the Joint Chiefs of Staff in 2015. Our regional commander, James Mattis, became Secretary of Defense. I never realized how legendary these men were, along with my lieutenant, Brian Chontosh, and my drill instructor, Sgt. Major Joe L. Vines, until I started working at Road Home. Reflecting later on, I was like, hey, I drank beers with these guys, we got into bar fights, we really did some stupid shit. These guys are now legends!

"We got the call and built our timelines. We were going to be one of the first units in. Early on in the mission, I remember looking up with MGVs,* bombs, and missiles flying. Rockets [flew] into Iraq before they blew the breach open and later, the berm. I was thinking that the second we go through the berm it's going to be just like our training, pull the ring, run through.

"We were in country a few hours when the president declared we were at war. We pushed north and took down the first two oil separation plants. There were no firefights really, a couple of shots, OK. Guys are putting their weapons into stacks, giving up, taking their clothes off with their arms raised. All right, this might be just a walk through. This war thing isn't going to be too bad.

"For the next four days, it was just a continuing push north towards Baghdad. We were leading on Highway One for the rest of the Marine Corps to follow. The night before March 25th, on one of the last fire watches on the 24th, I remember breaking open an MRE looking for the

---

* The Future Combat Systems Manned Ground Vehicles (MGV) was a family of lighter and more transportable ground vehicles developed by BAE Systems Inc. and General Dynamics as part of the United States Army's Future Combat Systems (FCS) program, https://www.onwar.com/weapons/afv/data/FCS-Manned-Ground-Vehicles.htm.

cheeseburgers. I hadn't had one yet, so at 5 a.m. I heated it up and stashed it under my seat. Totally void of any moisture, you add hot water and as described, they are ready to eat. On a personal note, they only taste good when you are extremely hungry and they have about three times the calories you'd expect. Then we get the call that we're moving out. We had one tank attached to us, that was our lead tank, four trucks in front of me a good distance behind, and eight trucks behind us, followed by the entire U.S. Marine Corps behind us.

"Five minutes later, we heard pops over the radio. Then, we got ambushed, like we hadn't moved. Even though it was what we prepared for, we had a mixture of emotions not really knowing what to expect. I had four gunners fired about ten feet from my truck and every other truck. It looked like a 4th of July Roman Candle fight, missiles flying everywhere.

"I have no idea how those gunners missed us, but they did. Ahead, there was heavy fire just laying into us. On the other side of the highway there were two mortar trucks just lobbing mortars at us and we were stuck in a kill zone.

"Our platoon commander who was in the lead element drove and ordered his truck to drive straight, right into the machine gun nest. In the truck in front of me was my roommate and my buddy who took an RPG* right into the chest plate. It exploded off of him and hit the corpsman in the backseat of my truck. We lost our corpsman.

"It happened right in front of me, there were lots of sparks, I probably saw it, I know it happened, but I just don't remember it. We kept on fighting, but it seemed like time just stopped. I had never experienced anything like that.

"You know that term 'the fog of war?' Well, it was there. There was stuff going on everywhere. We took one KIA.† My buddy who took the initial hit got pretty banged up, but he still serves in the Marine Corps as a drill sergeant.

"Shortly after the attack, I finally go to eat that cheeseburger, the best damn cheeseburger I ever had. But pretty quickly, we got caught in what was referred to as 'the 100-year sandstorm.' I had never seen anything like it. I had seen sandstorms before in Twentynine Palms [California] and in Arizona, but I had never seen anything like this. It was apocalyptic. The sky was red. There was sand everywhere, you couldn't see anything. At night

---

* Rocket-propelled grenades are an explosive projectile weapon used by many armies across the world. They play a major role in contemporary warfare and are also frequently used by insurgent and terrorist groups, https://science.howstuffworks.com/rpg.htm.

† Killed in action.

time, everything just went black, pitch black. I put my hand in front of my face and I couldn't see it. Then it got a little light again, which was weird, then it was back to lights out. It was so bad, we had to circle and tether the trucks so that we could walk and not get lost. The tank optics could only see twenty feet in front of them. Then the rumors started. There were stories that this large Iraqi tank battalion was coming for us and it was our mission to find them. I don't even know if it ever existed.

"After the storm, the next morning when I woke up, the chaplain came by to see if we were alright. And we were all looking into each other's eyes and that was the first time I really got a glimpse of PTSD or trauma or that thousand-yard stare. I'll never forget the look in everyone's faces. Everyone changed [*snaps his fingers*] instantly overnight.

"For the next forty-five to fifty days, we were in some type of firefight. Every day I slept maybe two hours. It was just drive until somebody shoots at you, then shoot back. Do it again. Repeat, repeat, repeat, repeat, repeat, repeat every day until we got to Baghdad. We damn near pushed up to the Iranian border. By the time we got where they were, [President] Bush got on the boat. War's over. So we ended up staying in the same town where the ambush took place, working with the same people that we were fighting against.

"It was a weird and interesting experience. My lieutenant was awarded the Navy Cross for taking out the machine gun nest and the effort for the following nine months, which was ironic because paperwork started coming in about discipline for the bar fight back in Spain.

"We never got shot at again. Iraq had changed, kids who spoke no English were now fluent. Brand-new Polo shirts, long skirts, and brand-new Huffy bikes were everywhere. We bought chicken from little kids in town. A Spanish army replaced us and shortly thereafter, the mortar attacks started—it was IED, IED, IED* everywhere.

"When I got back, it was time for us to leave the service. I had six months left, had saved up some money, had seven months to figure out the rest of my life. I did a lot of talking with my buddies and I knew I would attend school in Scottsdale, Arizona. My dream job was to be a beat writer for a minor-league baseball team, eat a hot dog, have a beer, write a story at the end of the night about what I saw. That sounded like a good life.

"In the meantime, all of my buddies who had their six months left, all went back to Iraq in a combat casualty replacement unit. I got orders

---

* IED stands for an improvised explosive device, used in unconventional ways. IEDs are commonly used as roadside bombs.

from March Air Force Base to become an urban warfare combat instructor. I didn't want to do it; all my best friends were going back to Iraq and there was no way in hell I was going to let them go back without me. I requested change of orders all the way up through generals ranks, and I was shot down at every level.

"It sucked and it led to shitty conversations with family members who couldn't understand. 'What are you doing? You're crazy. Why would you want to go back there? It doesn't make any sense. Just do your job and get out.' My buddies went back and did their job. They came home. We all got out. That six-month separation kind of put a rift between us. It sucked. Their experiences changed and so did mine.

"My transition preparation began with telling me that since I had started in California my unemployment rate was $1700/month, the best in the country. Then use your GI Bill where you can make $30,000–40,000 a year, just by going to school. I don't feel as if I was set up to succeed at all. It was awful, awful advice. At the time, I tried to use the VA and other support services and there wasn't any.

"Remember, I was the first group of service members to leave the military after a combat experience not seen since the Viet Nam War. I had spent nine months over there and people were looking at me like, 'Who are you? What are you doing?'

"Nobody was discussing PTSD, nobody was talking about the need to support the troops. Organizations like Wounded Warrior and other types of programs didn't exist. They just weren't there. There was only the VA and a few programs and maybe the VFW and American Legion where you could go have a beer and smoke some cigarettes.

"I was struggling to find work. I was doing retail work in the middle of the night, counting Victoria Secret lingerie at two o'clock in the morning. I'm like 'what am I doing.' This is miserable, I'm making $8/hour. This sucks.

"I had no idea what I was doing. I was in a fog. I was just proceeding according to plan until I could go to school and use my GI bill. I ended up using my GI bill as financial support while I got my degree, instead of using it to get my degree [*laughs*]. School in Scottsdale was easy. I carried a 4.0 GPA, two years straight. I was active, which really helped. Wrote on the student newspaper. After two years, I was accepted to the Journalism Department at Syracuse, which is like being accepted to the Harvard equivalent for journalism.

"Before heading for Syracuse, I spent the summer in Kentucky, where I started to reflect. OK, I'm going to school in Syracuse, I'm going to be

$120,000 in debt for two years. After graduation, if I'm lucky, I'll be a beat writer for a single or double AA team in the middle of nowhere Nebraska. I'll be making $20,000/yr. at best, just so I can drink a beer and have a hot dog? It's not adding up, it just doesn't make sense. The more generous post–9/11 bill wasn't yet available, which would have been a game changer. I had to cancel Syracuse. I wanted to go, but I think I just got cold feet. So I stayed in Kentucky. I didn't know what I was doing. I was not motivated, no reason to be motivated. I figured if I take enough community college classes I got money to live on.

"I spent the next eighteen months getting drunk with my buddy and going sailing. Every day. Wake up, go to the river, get on the boat, get drunk having a great time with my old high school buddy. He and my family lived within a five-minute walk to each other. My buddy was a high functional alcoholic, so I said, hey, I can do this too. Sounds like fun. What's not to like? I'm getting paid, got money in my pocket, and I can drink boat drinks at 11 a.m. and nobody says anything to me. I did this for a year. I just started drinking more and more until I, too, became a 24 hr./day high functioning alcoholic.

"I started to get into trouble. My money went away because I stopped going to school. And I said, what am I doing? I'm twenty-six years old and now I've gone back to what I was doing when I was nineteen. I basically had six years of arrested development with some wild experiences around the world. I was hitting rock bottom and bouncing off of it. I found myself living in the back of my Jeep, isolating myself from my family. My family would go to work, so I would go to the house, shower, hang out, and before they came back home, I would leave and then go out to party. We never saw each other, I just used their house. It just wasn't working.

"My dad helped me find the local VA. I had some conversations, we didn't connect, they gave me meds, and I thought, 'Great! More stuff to party with. Alright!' I began mixing barbiturates and alcohol and maybe I wouldn't wake up, which had happened to a buddy of mine. My sister helped get me a job in her hospital, working sort of as an orderly to kids aged three to thirteen with some severe behavioral problems. I worked with kids, and since I was a fit Marine, my job was to run around, chase kids, put them in restraints, so I was always on call. It wasn't bad. It was a good paycheck, and started to give me some purpose.

"I always was a good cook. At fourteen, I was working at Subway and pizza places. There was a fantastic culinary school in Louisville. I went there and I loved it, or at least I thought I did. I still was getting only thirty minutes to two hours of sleep a night. I was out partying and then I'd wake up and go to school. While I was there, I met my future wife. I liked her immediately and we had a similar fun lifestyle. I was either going to end up in the hospital I worked at, or dead, but as luck would have it, she got pregnant. We moved to Chicago, got married, had a baby, and for the next seven months I tried to figure out what to do.

"My partying lifestyle continued. My alcohol consumption was out of control. In Kentucky, it kind of comes out of the tap, but in Chicago, I found clever ways of hiding bottles. I was working full time cooking at the Crown Hotel. Then I started skipping out of school and work, and just hid in my car four to five hours a day.

"I ended up at Hines VA in their inpatient program. I wasn't like the others around me. The drinking for me was hidden by working in a kitchen, but for four to five years, I'd drink heavily to knock myself out so I could sleep for two hours. I got out and didn't have a drink for eighteen months, started going to twelve-step AA meetings on a daily basis, hating every minute of it, feeling like it was some sort of penance.

"I got a job at a kitchen in Barrington, Illinois. I was making more money, not drinking, and getting my life back on track and repairing those relationships, which took a long time. Got interested in sushi so I took a job at Mariano's grocery as a chef. I was full time sushi now and was doing well. I had two young kids and working until two in the morning just wasn't working. I wanted to see my kids.

"I wish I didn't spend so much time [living like it was a] weekend at Bernie's, and I was Bernie. We were flat broke. Dirt broke. I had no income while I was an inpatient and I was between jobs. My wife, who works in sales, went to a food pantry in Palatine. Nancy, who worked there, noticed my wife, her professional clothing, nice car, said, 'You don't look like our other clients.' When they asked her why she was there, she told them, 'My husband's a vet, we have two kids and no money.' My wife began calling and calling Illinois veterans support organizations, but she was getting no answers.

"Finally, my wife found Mary Beth Beiersdorf and Salute, Inc.* and they helped us get back on our feet. We got daycare, other types of support. Salute, Inc. changed our lives. My wife and I, always thankful for the support we got, had on our minds that once we got settled, we would give back. I'm working at Road Home doing just that.

"I have no regrets, except with myself. I was and continue to be living the American Dream. It's a land of opportunity and it sounds totally cliché, but it's so true. I joined the Marine Corps. I travelled around the world. I

---

* https://www.saluteinc.org/.

got to see crazy things. I sat on top of the Babylon ruins, I've seen things that no one will ever see. That's irreplaceable.

"When I got out, I had my college paid for; there was VA hospitals out there, and now that there are programs, I can do whatever I want. There are internships for everything. There's EN-Abled Veteran Internship, there's Bunker Labs if you want to start your own business, go do it, it's right there. If I want to go back to cooking, I can do that.

"It's just a matter of getting out of the rearview mirror. I think that's one of the biggest challenges for vets; they're stuck in the rearview mirror. I talk to other vets who say, when we were in the Army doing this, when we were in Iraq doing that, when we were in Afghanistan, and it's all this backward-looking approach. They're stuck in the rearview mirror. That's why I really don't keep in touch with my buddies. After a few do you re-members, I get sleep paralysis that lasts for weeks. It's unfortunate, but these encounters put me back in the rearview mirror. I regret [not] spending time with my old buddies, but it's what's best for me.*

"Once I figured out how to knock that off, chuck that out and rec-oncile with my past, then I could look forward as to what I wanted to be in five months, a year, two years. Now I'm looking forward. Now I've got goals. Now I've got something to work towards. Now I created the purpose that I needed.

"My advice? For those transitioning back to civilian life, find mean-ing and purpose as soon as possible. Find something you like to do, try to figure out who you want to be. Set goals, set lots of goals, short term and long term, bounce them off buddies, then go after them. Find meaning and purpose outside of a bar.

"For family members, give all the support you can. Keep giving. I wanted to live. Without family support, I would be in prison or dead. They knew me before I joined the Marines, they knew me after. They knew when something was off as they were the ultimate baseline measure. At the VA, you can run all the qualitative measures you want, but you're not going to get that baseline your family provides.

"I found the right therapist in Evanston, Illinois, who helped me a lot. She had similar experiences and we made a connection. I didn't have to

---

* In 2014, a reunion of sorts was coordinated with embedded Fox News. Reporters held a ten-year reunion via Skype. "It was like getting the old rock band back together. But instead of Crosby, Stills and Nash, it was Chontosh, McIntosh, Burgwald, Jelinek, and South, and instead of joining together on stage, the reunion took place via Skype." (Greg Palkot, "The Making of 'Fal-lujah . . . Ten Years On,'" *Fox News*, November 13, 2014, accessed September 23, 2017, http://www.foxnews.com/us/2014/11/13/reporter-notebook-making-fallujah10-years-on.html). Chris Miller was not at this reunion.

unpack 90 percent of my bags. I didn't have to spend two sessions explaining that it was 140 degrees. I didn't have to explain to her where I was. She knew. So it took a while and when it clicked, that's huge.

"When you get out of the rearview mirror, you're not going back there, you're not going back in time, you're not going back to your buddies you served with, you're not going back to any of the countries, you're not going back to the Marine Corps. What's next? Look forward. Start planning. If it helps to do it in the military fashion, do it in the military fashion. Whatever methods the services taught you on how to take initiative and move forward, use them.

"I got taught all the skills I ever needed in the Marine Corps infantry. I got to blow up lots of stuff and shoot tanks. There are skills in there you can translate; it just takes a little work. I was able to translate the things I've done in my past to better my future. And I think everyone who has served in the military has that skill set.

"Asking for help was the hardest thing I had to do. I'd rather go into combat than to ask for help, and of course, the Marines reinforce this. I've got this. I can figure this out. I slept in a hole in the ground for nine months. I can sleep anywhere. All the while I thought 'I got this.' I am totally comfortable sleeping in a swamp with mosquitoes. A veteran's rock bottom is very very low. I've been through it all and no challenge could be worse than what I've been through.

"The best thing about me and the last four years at Road Home Program is I have a place to help other veterans ask for help. For me, asking for help is the toughest thing I'll ever do, so if I can ease that burden for other veterans, that's huge."

4

WHEN INNOCENCE AND
THE INNOCENTS DIE

*And I don't feel good about it. Because there's not enough reason,
man, to feel a person die in your hands or to see your best buddy get
blown away. I'm here to tell you, it's a lousy thing, man. I don't see
any reason for it. And there's a lot of shit that I did over there that
I find fucking hard to live with. And I don't want to see people like
you, man, coming back and having to face the rest of your lives with
that kind of shit. It's as simple as that.*[1]

—Luke's speech (Jon Voight), in *Coming Home* (1978)

War is the most brutal aspect of human existence. War encompasses
all that is evil in the world—death, torture, excruciating pain, rape,
dismemberment, and sorrow—in the name of an ideology, government,
or religion. Its scars extend beyond the warfighter to family, friends, and
colleagues. The act of going to war is often decided by those who do not
go to fight and, perhaps, never donned a uniform. But for those who do
go, the complexities and mistakes made during war can be widespread and
last a lifetime.

Such is the story of Dwaine Goings, a man I hired as a software en-
gineer at Rush University Medical Center. We hired him based upon his
experience and talent. Dwaine was an Army Ranger in Black Hawk Down,
which he never really wanted to talk about. I respected his privacy and after
I asked him once about it, I never asked again.

"When I joined the Army in 1986, I went to combat with the 82nd
Airborne in Honduras and Panama. In 1988, I was in Panama, which was
my first combat experience. I was a forward observer, infantry man. Our
objective was to take down the airfield and the airfield tower. We experienced small arms fire as we moved towards the tower. When my buddy and

I knocked down the door, we stormed the building and shot two enemy in the stairwell. We lit up the staircase and they came tumbling down. We made it to the top to the tower to call in air support. That was my first experience in combat, and that was something else. All that training just kicked in.

"After Panama, I was back at Ft. Bragg and was in training at Ft. Smith, Arkansas. While we were there, Saddam Hussein started acting up. One day while President Bush was talking, we flew back to Ft. Bragg where we re-geared and got on a civilian 747 reconfigured for combat headed for Iraq. We were all sittin' on top of all our ammo. If somebody hit our plane that would've been a pretty big bang in the air [*laughs*].

"When we got there, man, it was hot! We moved toward the border to make our line in the sand where Saddam could not cross. The Republican Guard did cross the line, but being the first ones there, they were outgunned.

"Our orders were, nothing moves at night. If it moves, we kill it. One night, on a Humvee, we got word that vehicles were moving from the north to the south, coming into our sector. With those orders in mind, I laid the guns on a preplanned target. Then, I was coming back to the scouts—did they identify whether the vehicles were friendly or foe?

"They kept coming back saying they didn't identify, they didn't identify. I really didn't want to fire unless I knew it was an enemy vehicle. Later our platoon sergeant drove up to my position. He kept telling me and telling me, you're going to fire the target and I kept telling him that I can't identify, I can't identify.

"At the same time, we had aircraft coming in. The Air Force got on the line and they told me they were three minutes out. So as these vehicles were moving and coming into sight over the horizon, I started doing my training drills to determine how fast they were travelling, get coordinates, stuff like that. I was getting the guns laid on and the aircraft lined up. We go into this thing called the nine line where we talk the aircraft right on to the target. While I was doing this, I asked my radio telephone operator to see if he could identify the target. He told me he couldn't.

"So I grabbed the scope myself to see, and I couldn't identify the target either. Meanwhile, I had the platoon sergeant yelling in my ear 'Fire the target, fire the target.' And I keep telling him, I can't identify, I can't identify. Remember now, the orders were if anything moves at night, kill it. I was given an ultimatum—if you don't fire on that target, you're going to be busted down to nothing. I laid the guns on kilo uniform 3200 (I'll never forget the name of that target), and I was talking to the aircraft. I lined up the aircraft and I gave them the all clear hot.

"They made a first swipe with one aircraft going high and the other going low because they always come in with antiaircraft. He comes down and he strafes the target with a M30 millimeter or M40 millimeter cannon, I forget, on the front of those things. You could see the road coming up, I mean he was lighting 'em up. As he egressed out, the second one comes around and he makes his strafe and run. They strafed the target three times. The convoy stopped, it was like six vehicles or something. They [aircraft] did their thing, and said they were bugging out.

"They started to leave but at the same time after they got done, I fired howitzers and dropped artillery on top of the vehicles. I dropped eighteen high explosive rounds, which blew a couple of vehicles, took a couple of them over, stuff like that. After I fired the eighteen rounds, I fired Wille P* to burn the target—make sure it doesn't move. Make sure it's dead, that's what we call it. Afterward, everyone congratulates each other and says that's a good kill. You did a good job.

"We didn't check out the target until the next day. We drove up to the target and as we got close, we started looking at the bodies. We noticed a couple of dead guys—they looked like they were running away from the vehicle but got mowed down, likely from the A-10 aircraft.

"Bad part was when we pulled back and opened up and started to look in the backseats of the vehicles, we found dead women and children. They were refugees trying to get away from the war. They didn't know. [*At this point, Dwaine takes a short pause.*] I was devastated. I didn't sign up to kill women and children. I signed up to kill the enemy. Me, the lieutenant, and the drill sergeant, we got into a big fight because I went off and said 'This is not happening.' I didn't do this. I couldn't believe this is what I did. I mean, I was going off.

"I was good at what I did. I was one of the best—got top gunner three years in a row. But I didn't sign up for this. I didn't sign up to do this, see-ing the devastation and stuff. These were just innocent people trying to get away, and it really hit me hard.

"I was fighting the lieutenant, I was fighting the platoon sergeant. They had to get me off to the side to get me to calm down. I know these things happen in war but these things still haunt me today. My radio telephone operator, he broke down and started crying, too. I mean, we just don't make mistakes like that. My biggest thing was you wouldn't let me identify. You wouldn't let me identify. After that, I took a very strong disliking to my

---

* A Wille P is a grenade that when explodes creates a cloud of white phosphorous, burning any flammables in its radius.

chain of command because [they] wouldn't let me identify. You made me do this. You MADE me do this. That's how I felt. You made me do this without going through the proper procedures. You made me do this.

"But, y'know, time goes on. I still [haven't] learned to live with it. I thought to myself, how can I go home? I killed innocent people. I'm a monster. It haunts me. It really haunts me.

"I finished out my duties as a leader of men, but I kept everything bottled up. When they were laughing, cracking jokes, I just had to walk away. I was a monster, man. We were doing horrible things to people. When you're out in the field, you just have to live with it.

"That's why I'm as fucked up as I am."

In my career, no one took more advantage of my open-door policy than Dwaine Goings. In the five years I have known him, not once has Dwaine called me by my first name. He either called me by rank, Colonel, or more often, Sir. To me, that a man of his caliber, a war-experienced senior Army Ranger, a bona fide hero, referred to me by rank only, was a huge thrill for me.

The love and respect was mutual. Well, the love is there on my side, maybe Dwaine needs a little more work to admit it's on his side, too.

During his employment, Dwaine was completely open about his PTSD, readily describing his Walgreen deep-dish daily medication dispenser. "Sir, I take one pill at this time of day, and see that, two others during the day. Well, I take that one later on, and before I go to bed, I take this pill, which knocks me out until morning." His medication regimen was quite impressive and seemed to work quite well, give or take some moments of excitement and enthusiasm. But I wasn't sure Dwaine knew what medication he was actually taking.

Along with information related to his military career and PTSD, he fully disclosed a felony conviction on his job application. The Human Resources Department had zeroed in on this disclosure and was sending me negative messages. When his resume came to me, I, too, saw why there were levels of concern. Things could have stopped right there, but I decided to give Dwaine a shot. I am fully aware of the questions you cannot ask during the interview process. I am very careful and follow the letter of the labor law very seriously. Anyway, here is how it went down.

"Dwaine, I gotta tell you, man. You have a very impressive resume with solid skills and experience. I am also impressed by your openness and full disclosure about your PTSD. Tell me about your career, including life after military service and this felony conviction you have openly disclosed on your application."

"Sir, I am a proud Army soldier who served his country honorably. As an Army Ranger, I am a veteran of Black Hawk Down, as well as many other operations, some of which are classified and others I just don't want to talk about. Because of my PTSD, I was medically boarded out at twenty years, given full retirement benefits, and a 100 percent service connected disability rating."

But there was a problem: Dwaine was a convicted felon. He explains how this came about.

"When I was interviewing, I said let me tell you about me, because I did time. I did do time. I remember the night I was sitting, when I was drinking to forget. I didn't want trouble but they caught me on a bad day. They caught me on one of my wanting to forget days. I was on my porch, in my own yard, my own thing. The cops came on my property and they were looking for someone else but they ran across me.

"They said 'Let see your ID' and I said 'you get out of my yard.' 'Well, you fit the description.' [So I said] 'I don't fit shit [*laughs*]. I will whoop your ass.' So we went at it and they found out they ran into the wrong Ranger. They came up still asking about ID, [saying] you look like our suspect. So as I'm walking back to my porch, one of them goes to grab me, which was the wrong thing he could have done. I came around, jacked him up, grabbed that leg, threw him down, BOOM.

"Ah, here comes his buddy. You want to come get some of this too? He got a flip, BOOM. Got him down. Went hand to hand combat with his club, knocked him down again. Went to the other cop, put his hands behind him and cuffed him with his own handcuffs. Did the same to the other cop.

"I could hear them talking into the radios, 'You gotta get over here, you gotta get over here. We need help!' I emptied their guns, shook the bullets to the ground, and I sat on the curb. I put my cigarette out and thought to myself, you know, I bet half of the entire Omaha police force is about to show up. And they did.

"So they came and did their thing, worked me over, handcuffed me, and put me in the car. They didn't charge me with nothing. They said, 'What's wrong with your knee?' I said I hurt my knee in the conflict. Well, we better get you to the hospital. No shit, I said.

"So I get to the emergency room in handcuffs along with the two cops. I'm leaning on one cop and he says you better get off me, you better get off me and he starts pushing me. I said don't push me, it's my knee. So he pushed me again and I said, 'If you think these handcuffs are gonna stop me, I whooped your ass in the front yard, I'll whoop your ass again.'

"'I'd like to see you' and before he got the rest out, I popped up the knee, it hurt like hell, but I popped up that knee and pushed him off but the other one was still hooked to me and he slammed me into the wall. I turned around to the other cop and got over him with my feet. The other cop got out his billy club like he was going to hit me.

"Just then the doctor came in and said, 'Don't you hit that man he's handcuffed.' I was handling their asses, sir. So I had whooped their asses again in front of all those people looking at us in the emergency room—*that's* when they charged me with assaulting a police officer.

"When we went to court, my mom was down there for some reason. And I could hear them talking and she was telling them, 'well, he's been through a lot in the war.' Other stuff I couldn't hear. So the prosecutor is agreeing with everything and I said, 'Wait, hold on! Include the part where I was handcuffed. So the judge goes to the prosecutor and says, 'Are you telling me that a half-drunk man in handcuffs was fighting with the police?' 'Well, yeah,' the prosecutor said. They went into chambers and the judge gave me thirty months. The first couple of months, they had to drive me every day to the VA for treatment. An Omaha corrections office had to get me up at 5:30 a.m., drive me to the VA, unhandcuff me, then I would go walk up, by myself, to the VA. Now, does that sound like a dangerous criminal to you?

"So I went through classes again, anger management and all that. At 7 p.m. they would take me back to jail where I would sleep. Then, we did it all over again the next day. After a while, they got tired of driving me back and forth so they put me on work release. Picking up trash and stuff. For thirty months, the only time I was in jail was when I was sleeping. I stayed and kept my head down because, like I said, I didn't want any trouble."

I asked Dwaine what he learned and what steps he had taken to avoid a recurrence of this event.

"Sir, I stay at home and don't go out at night no more. In my apartment, I have everything in the order I like. My clothes are hung up and aligned just the way I like it. There is not a spot of dirt anywhere, including bathrooms and sinks. I cook my own meals and I spend my evenings in front of two computer monitors continuing to learn as much about technology as I possibly can.

"I still drink my twelve-pack every night, but I'm happy and safe and when I take my sleeping pill, I am out like a light until it's time to go to work."

I took what I guess could be described as a "pregnant pause." I'm not a psychiatrist but I do know that mixing alcohol with antidepressants is not a good idea, whether you decide to stay indoors or not.

I said to him, "You know, Dwaine, I'm not a doctor, nor do I play one on TV, but from what you described, I believe a twelve-pack of beer is going to act as a depressant, which may counteract with any antidepressants that you may be taking. So how does that work for you?" I will never forget the sincerity and conviction of his answer.

"Sir, I'm an Army Ranger. I smoke cigarettes and drink beer, and that's what I do."

When I interview engineers there is a certain quality I look for that is difficult for me to describe. I depend heavily upon my experiences, gut reaction, and my ability to read people's hearts, not just their words and mind.

I looked hard and long into Dwaine's eyes, all the while processing the unorthodox treatment plan I heard and the heart I had seen. What I saw was a man of value, dedication, character, sense of service, and a continuing drive to improve himself and continue his service without the uniform. Whatever medication he was taking was working.

I looked at him sternly, raised my right hand to my right temple palm down and saluted. "Carry on, soldier."

What else could I do? This man not only understood his disability, he was not ashamed of it. He recognized what he had to do to build a mitigation strategy that minimized risk and maximized his capabilities, and he did it. It certainly wasn't a conventional approach and not something I would recommend to anybody, but it worked for him.

Dwaine had the discipline to stick with it as well as the honesty to provide full deployment disclosure, unashamed of the mistakes he made but radiant in his confidence in purpose and willingness to continue to serve. I respectively took human resource's recommendations under advisement and hired him anyway. I saw what I saw and was determined to hire this man.

Turns out, my hunch was right. Dwaine was a great employee. Yes, he had some qualities different from other engineers, but his work effort, passion for his team and patients, and his hard work ethic stepped up the game of those around him.

Oh sure, I heard some terms, "that guy," "he's crazy," "man, oh man," and so on. But nobody questioned his work ethic, his knowledge, nor his dedication to the team and its mission. Things were going quite well—I would hire him again in a minute.

5

A GOLD STAR MOM'S PTSD

The telegram came crashing
To senses dealt a most devastating,
Horrible blow.
This contentious war
Had laid her beloved son low.
Fallen was the son nurtured at her breast
Fighting far, far away
At his countries [sic] *behest*[1]

—Excerpt from "A Mother Lost Her Son to War"
by Gary Jacobson

PTSD does not just happen in war. Physical abuse, rape, childhood neglect, robbery, and other events that severely damage a person physically or emotionally can trigger PTSD. The indelible scars left behind from a horrific event changes a person dramatically. This includes mothers and fathers of the fallen, as well.

The term *Gold Star Mom* applies to any mother who has lost a child who was serving in the U.S. Armed Forces. Certain provisions are made for stepmothers, grandmothers, and other family members, including husbands, grandparents, or others, who were instrumental in raising and providing for the military member. American Gold Star Mothers, Inc. is the governing body supporting its members through counselling, advocacy, and other support services.[2]

I met a woman who, from the outside, looks like your typical Midwestern mom. Enormously talented in art and graphics, Modie Lavin ran her own graphic arts business for many years.

"I was born and bred Chicago native, Southside of Beverly. We have strong roots there; my dad went to the same school system as I. For many years, I made my living in decorative arts and owned my own business. My specialty is with murals and other types of paintings and art. My two beautiful children, Conner Lowry from my first husband and my daughter Grace Lavin from my second husband. As life would have it, I found myself a single mother. We lived in a beautiful home in Beverly. I had a thriving, wonderful business. Conner went off to high school, a Catholic School and had a really good time. He's a wonderful boy; he did great at Brother Rice. He had a little too much freedom, however, and along with a couple of friends, he called me up one day and said, 'Mom, guess what? Me and my friends just enlisted in the Marine Corps.'

"Now, I have no military brats in my family; and with this news, you could have knocked me over with a feather. Like any typical mother, I was not happy about it, but I understood that Conner needed to find his own path since high school was not working out. So off he goes and gets ready. His sister Gracie and I met him at the MEPS station at O'Hare airport, the first step to bootcamp. Understand, we have a very close family relationship. Today it became clear that Conner was not himself and even the people around us were picking up on the fact that Conner was not very stable. Emotionally he was kind of showing cracks on the outside. He was given the opportunity to not go through with this, but his response was, 'No turning back now.'

"Still, he wouldn't let me and Gracie go. All of the other families had left after they took the oath except us; we were down in the hallway waiting for the bus to take him to the plane. Me and his sister had tight grips around his waist. Mind you, Conner was 6'5" tall. He whispered into my ear, 'Mom, please don't cry' as his own tears were falling on my face.

"We were kind of a spectacle as all these other Marines, whose families had left, were all watching us. The bus came and we said, 'You gotta go,' but he still wouldn't let go of us. Finally, he went out to get on the bus. And so, we turned and left and were making our way out. Gracie being young, said, 'Mom, he's going down the wrong way. We gotta catch him.' And I said, 'I can't turn around, Grace. We've got to go to the car now.'

"It started raining and Gracie fell asleep in the backseat. I drove home with the windshield wipers on, no radio on, no other sound, and I just cried, knowing I had just kinda gave my son away, in a sense, and it wasn't like a marriage, this was the military.

"From bootcamp, the letters home we received were so profound and full of love. You couldn't stop me in a grocery store without me carrying on about my son preparing for the Marine Corp. We flew out for graduation, where, my son, always the leader, ended up being a squad leader. This boy that slid down the wall a few months ago, now walked proudly out on the parade deck like a peacock in formation.

"When the ceremony ended and he got the release, it was me knocking down people and he doing the same as we were trying to get to each other. We started clutching each other and he started crying . . . again. The same way I left him [*laughs*]. But now, he was a Marine.

"He proceeded on with his tour of duty. Through letters we stayed in touch. For the first eighteen months, he hated the Marine Corps. 'I can't do this. This sucks.' He went on to win some leadership medals and about three years into the Marines, he was getting ready to go to Afghanistan. Now Conner started feeling it. Now he's a United States Marine. Let's go get some.

"He didn't have to go. He volunteered to go. He went over there and instantly was put in a leadership role. And that was a very difficult time for me. I knew he was going into a warzone, but this is my only son! In the back of my mind, I was always thinking, 'This isn't going to happen to me. Nobody is going to take my Conner away from me.' And I was his queen. I was his number one girl. It was hard for him as he knew he was hurting me going over there.

"He got there November 1st and thirty days later, a staff sergeant stepped on an IED right next to Conner. Conner was awarded the Bronze Star for Valor. After that incident, there was this monotone in his voice that came out whenever I talked to him. As a mom, I knew he had changed overnight.

"After that, every phone call, every letter was about 'just get[ting] the hell home.' He confided he had worries. He was scared. At one point when he called, about ten days before he died, he said, 'Mom, you should have seen the beauty of the mountainside here. It's the most beautiful thing I have ever seen in my life.' And he was carrying on about this and I'm thinking, 'You're in a warzone!'

"About a week later, there was an incident about Koran burning. Conner called and told me that all of the Afghan National Army had been kicked off the base. When I asked him why, he said, 'Because they're trying to kill Marines.'

"We did our usual I love you. Stay safe. Be careful. Stuff we said a thousand times. 'I've seen this stuff on the news. Be careful.' We hung up at one o'clock in the morning. The next day, March 1, 2012, at one o'clock in the afternoon, a Marine detail was on my front porch.

"Seeing them was like being in a high-speed head-on car crash, suffering multiple, invisible, but still life-threatening injuries. I knew my life was over. The understanding that I got was that Conner was on a mission on a Humvee; from my understanding corporals are not supposed to be. But even at his height, and being a lance corporal, he was there. He was there because he is Conner Thomas Lowry.

"Going in everything was fine and they took the same path out. But on the way back, there was a low hanging wire, kind of a result of kicking the Afghan Army off the base.

"They pulled over, and he was in bad shape. They called in a helicopter and they worked on him for twenty-three minutes. A year later, the helicopter medic sent me this amazing letter with a blow by blow about having Conner on board with him and the impact it had on the team once they got to the MASH unit. He guaranteed me that Conner was killed instantly. He didn't suffer. And after a year later, it's never left him either. So I have somebody whom I have never met was carrying this with him a year later. And I continue to get letters from all over the world.

"Conner's death destroyed me. It destroyed me. I had to seek out mental health services; I knew I needed help. Today, I have found my way to the Road Home Program. Here, selfishly, I am a family outreach coordinator. I need to keep busy. Thinking of others in pain, helping others in pain, sharing my pain, and benefitting others is what I do. It's a wonderful journey that Conner has had every bit to do with.

"When Conner's unit returned at the end of May 2012 they flew me to San Diego for a military service there. It was an amazing memorial on the parade deck at Camp Pendleton. I got to meet his buddies and we got to know each other a little bit with a magnificent view of the ocean while we talked. I started the Conner T. Lowry memorial fund and now these men have come in every year for the last five years. We remain really tight on Facebook and stuff like that.

"What I learned was that Conner's death affected his unit very deeply. The looks on their faces when they first saw me? They were terrified. Conner talked about his mom a lot and they just didn't know what to expect from me. It took about an hour for them to start to feel better around me. At the end of the evening, a couple of them broke down and apologized profusely to me. I got a lot of 'I let you down, it should have been me,' stuff like that. I was taken aback, but I never imagined any of this. They are suffering too as this will be with them the rest of their lives. All of them felt incredibly guilty, yeah . . . yeah. A couple couldn't look at or speak to me. After a few years, I would get a phone call from one of the silent ones who would call and apologize for not making a relationship earlier. I said it was OK. Sometimes, it takes time.

"I was diagnosed with PTSD. I had a problem trying to live. The loss of a child in any capacity is too much to handle. It's not a natural normal process losing a child. Gracie was also affected deeply and it was a challenge getting her through the University of Wisconsin at Madison this year. Her mental health was deeply affected as well. My daughter is suffering from anxiety, depression, not understanding her emotions any more, and is going through deep therapy.

"I've learned to be able to open up and share. I kinda get it. I get trauma and I get mental health and I get what happens with war in the household. I always preface my outreach with the fact that my mental health was challenged prior to when Conner was killed, both mine and Gracie's. The stress of my son going into the Marine Corps and being in Afghanistan just levelled me. I felt depression slipping in. This just wasn't normal. This is not in the playbook.

"Today, I go to communities and create awareness of PTSD and other invisible wounds of war to other families. I'm not a clinician, but I am called upon by clinicians, so hopefully, by telling my story, at least one person attending the outreach program will hear my story and want to seek treatment. And if I do make a connection we have an intake.

"My job is the preservation of the family. The Road Home Program brings veterans into Chicago for three weeks in their Intensive Outpatient Program (IOP). In the last week, family members may join. Hopefully, we make a connection and trust can begin, which is so important in treatment. Most of the people that go through IOP have PTSD. But I also have connected with other Gold Star families. A lot of the PTSD I see is based around the loss of their battle buddies. I also meet families who are feeling the PTSD in their families and with all the trauma, guilt, shame, sleeping on the floor, etc. that goes with it. Some families are close to separating. Others are close to divorce.

"None of us are really equipped to deal with PTSD, I mean, what is it, 1 percent serve and of that only 1 percent serve in combat. This is a rarity. I've learned that when treated, you can keep going and that's what we are doing. Make sure everybody in the household knows what PTSD is and that everyone in the household knows how to have a conversation. This is just part of the treatment that Road Home provides.

"It hurts and it will continue to hurt. But I came out the other side and I hope to inspire other families that they, too, can do the same."

God bless the Lavin family.

II

NEW STRATEGIES FOR TRANSITIONING VETERANS

6

A SENSE OF PURPOSE

"Here comes the general" and they all say "General who?"
They're delighted that he came
But they can't recall his name
Nobody thinks of assigning him
When they stop wining and dining him
It seems this country never has enjoyed
So many one and two and three and four star generals
Unemployed[1]

—"What Can You Do with a General"
(Irving Berlin, *White Christmas*, 1954)

Military life is full of purpose: the ability to serve, the responsibility of defending the country and promoting peace, the role the member plays in those noble causes, and so on. It is difficult for that military veteran to find that same sense of purpose upon returning home. Many of the civilian jobs that are available don't provide a satisfactory level of responsibility or service.

Pete was a civilian dentist who, in his mid-fifties, decided he wanted to do his part to fight the war on terror. Age is not a factor if the military needs your specialty. The military often needs dentists, regardless of age, not just for clinical expertise, but also for their maturity and versatility. Pete did get a chance to do dentistry in Iraq. His most common patients? Dogs.

"Sure, I did some regular dentistry and some reconstruction work," he told me. "But most of that occurred behind the lines. The dogs, man, they needed work. I had worked on cadavers in college, but nothing like a dog. I got to be pretty good at fixing and pulling their teeth. I think [the] smiles I improved, though, were the ones from the handlers!"

"I did a lot of basic stuff, stitches, head wounds, like that. Because I was an Army major, I was also platoon leader for about four hundred people. I got a lot of responsibility real fast! I also saw some really bad stuff. Remember that day I made you walk around the Coke can [*nervous laughter*]? Well, there's a lot of cans over there."

I asked Pete about his transition home.

"Well, it wasn't easy and I'm still working through it. I can tell you with 100 percent certainty that it was easier for me to deploy to Iraq than it was for me to come home. They threw me a great party when I got back. All my family and friends and we had a great time. But that didn't last very long. Let me give you some examples.

"The Monday after I got back, I saw my wife making out the bills. I said to her, 'Hey, Honey. I can do the bills now. I got time and besides, I used to do the family finances.' Her reply? 'Oh, that's OK, Pete. Don't worry about it. We have a new filing system now, and besides, a lot of the bills are paid online. You take it easy, Pete, you've been through a lot. Just give yourself some time.'

"What did I hear? 'Our household has moved on without you.'

"Then, I would see my daughter. When I left, she was fourteen. When I came back, she's fifteen, has a lot of metal studs on her ears, a driver's permit, and a boyfriend named, I kid you not, Thor. I say her to her, 'Honey, you've grown up so fast. I'm not sure about this guy Thor.' She comes back with, 'Well, Daddy, I've grown up! Where've you been?'

"What did I hear? My daughter doesn't respect me!

"Then, I go play cards with my buddies. Talk turns to 'Can you believe I had to wait fifteen minutes at McDonald's this morning?' 'My boss is driving me crazy.' 'My golf game really sucks.'

"Jaime, I can't deal with this stuff. This is crap. These guys are worried about all this stupid stuff. So you know what they say, 'C'mon Pete. Lighten up, man. You're safe. You're back in the good ol' USA! Have another beer! Where's the old Pete?'

"I can't even relate to my friends anymore."

"So, what are you doing now, Pete?" I asked.

"Drinking," he said. "First I drank at night so I could sleep. Now, I start drinking before noon."

"You know that's not the answer," I told him.

"I know," he said. "But it's only temporary. I went back to my unit and told them I wanted to go back. I leave in two weeks to go back to Iraq."

"Wow," I said. "I guess that's pretty good. What does your family think?"

"I don't care," he said, shaking his head. "There's nothing I can do here. It's nobody's fault. I used to be in charge of 250 people. I helped off board ambulances, comfort soldiers, set up tents, coordinated with other units. I proudly served my country. I had a purpose. I had a lot of people depending upon me. I loved it. Now, I just sit around my condo all day long. Can't find a job, hate TV, and I'd rather drink alone. I know I can't keep doing this, Jaime. But I'm not the same person I used to be and nobody seems to understand that."

The wave of goodwill coming home is ephemeral.

As a PhD candidate in sociocultural anthropology at the University of Washington, Anna Zogas has done extensive research in the area of military transition. Here are her thoughts on the military transition process:

> During the United States' post-9/11 wars, the American public has been presented with many overly simplified stories of how the wars affect US service members. Media accounts of troops who survive combat often highlight the devastating effects of physical and psychological trauma, and instances when the government has failed to provide adequate care for injured veterans.
>
> Young veterans regularly observe that the military does an extremely effective job of training them to operate within the military, and an extremely poor job of reversing that training or preparing them before sending them back into civilian life.[2]

And according to Rasmussen Reports,

> Of the many hurdles military veterans face in America today, they name adjusting back to everyday life as the most significant challenge. Many also fell that private companies are not making the adjustment any easier. A new RallyPoint/Rasmussen Reports national survey of active and retired military personnel finds that 38% consider the transition back to civilian life to be the most significant challenge facing veterans today.[3]

Michael B. Brennan, PsyD, ABPP, is associate clinical director, Intensive Outpatient Program at the Rush Road Home Program. "While on active duty, military personnel are used to a highly structured environment. Military life includes a clear change of command, rank structure, thousands of operating structures which include military procedures as well as a code of conduct. Our military members have a clear identity, it starts with the name on the chest, rank on the solder boards, medals and citations on the uniform and a well understood code of conduct.

"Military members serve 24/7 and their actions outside of the base are just as important as same actions while on duty. When a service member leaves the service, oftentimes there are false expectations. Civilian life looks pretty good! The grass is always greener, there is no real change of command, I can wear what I want and cut my hair the way I want to, etc.

"What quickly happens is that the military member doesn't find that green grass. The first loss is the loss of identity and this happens in different ways. First, regardless of the period of time served, a military member has an identity in the branch of service they serve. Items related to that identity are no longer applicable: the base pay, uniform, military housing, comradery, social clubs are suddenly all gone, and there is nothing there to immediately replace these things.

"The second loss relates to the lack of a transition game plan. Ironically, as structured as military life is, there is no real structure and great variation in terms of what the transition strategy is and how does it start? How do I articulate what I did to a less structured and disciplined job environment? The services and the VA do not have a coordinated transition methodology. Consequently, a lot of veterans fall through the cracks due a lack of cohesive strategy. Lastly, transitioning veterans are told some things that are simply not true and is not a good formula for success."

In a recent report from the University of Washington, Zogas describes the difficulties military veterans face upon leaving military service.

> The basic idea that veterans must embark on a "transition" as they move from military to civilian life has been central for researchers, doctors, policy-makers, and activists thinking about the physical, emotional, and social experiences of post-9/11 veterans. There are advantages and disadvantages to describing these consequences as a transition.
>
> "Transition" provides an alternative to "trauma," promotes a comprehensive view of veterans' post-military difficulties, and it has been used to encourage veterans to seek help in spite of recalcitrant stigmas surrounding mental health concerns such as post-traumatic stress disorder (PTSD). At the same time, a focus on individual veterans' personal processes of change or growth risks obscuring the fact that veterans' post-military lives are connected to larger political organizational, and economic contexts.[4]

In her book *Battle Buddy: Maneuvering the Battlefield of Transitioning from the Military,* retired Chief Warrant Officer Lila Holley describes her experience coming home from service:

I was literally caught off guard by the emotional challenges faced during my transition from military life to civilian life after my 22-year career in the military. As I inquired of others who had transitioned before me and those in my peer group who had yet to face transition, I soon discovered this was a normal reaction—there was nothing strange about what I was experiencing. It was just new to me, something I had to figure out for myself like those before me.

What I learned along this journey is that every Service Member's transition experience differs because of the individual, life experiences, personal goals following military service, and the ability to process emotions tied to transitioning.[5]

Other veterans, like Army Sergeant Demetrice Barnes, face life after the military having been exposed to harmful chemical agents during deployment. "I loved the military. Sometimes I regret getting out. I wish I could have stayed longer. But due to some medical things that happened to me after a military deployment and after being exposed to some type of chemical during a deployment, my reflexes stopped working and my pupils stopped reacting to light. I had some other medical things that happened to me, which forced the military to medically retire me after eleven years of service.

"Initially I was medically retired from the Army with 60 percent service connected disability. But because of the severity of my disability, I was moved to 100 percent service connected disability within one year from the VA. Because I could no longer perform the duties the Army had trained me to do, I applied for vocational rehabilitation and was given the opportunity to go back to school to get a dual bachelor's degree in psychology and social work. I then got a master's degree in counselling and psychology from Texas A&M and I am a PhD candidate in psychology preparing to defend my thesis.

"My thesis is based upon the experience of female veterans returning home who had to leave their children while they were deployed in a combat situation. I'm looking forwarding to defending that in the near future and having the findings published in one of the psychology journals. My baby was four months old when I had to leave her and I want society to understand what female veterans have to endure when some of us have to leave our children as young as three months.

"You know how you always feel when you are at your lowest of lows. Doing what I was doing I was able to meet people, not that it was a gratification in meeting people that were doing worse, but to think that there was no way that there were people that were struggling as much as I was. There were people in situations worse off than I was, which gave me a new appreciation of where I was. To have people come into my office and find out they were worse off than I was gave me a newfound appreciation for what I had and it motivated me even more to assist these individuals. At least I had a meal in front of me. It might not have been a steak and a baked potato but I had a chicken leg and some potatoes that I could boil and make a meal out of."

Gayle Tzemach Lemmon is a senior fellow at the Council on Foreign Relations and is the author of the *New York Times* best seller *Ashley's War: The Untold Story of a Team of Women Soldiers on the Special Ops Battlefield* (2015). She offers her perspective in a piece for the *Los Angeles Times*:

> Since 9/11, more than 200,000 women have been deployed to Iraq and Afghanistan, and more than 160 women have died in service to their country. Women have fought on the front lines as combat pilots and military police platoon leaders. They have received Silver Stars and Bronze Stars for Valor. Some have even joined special operations forces on combat missions. Yet when people think of veterans, they rarely think of women.
>
> As the veteran's organization, the Mission Continues, found in a survey out this week of female veterans, a "common theme among our respondents was a perception of invisibility both in the service and at home. While in uniform, nearly two-thirds of respondents said they had to work harder than men to prove themselves. When those women left the military, barely a third (37%) said they felt recognized, respected and valued by society for their contributions as veterans."[6]

Lemmon continues:

> One veteran in Minnesota told me recently that when she tried to join a local veteran's organization, she was guided to the women's auxiliary rather than the group for service members. Another soldier based at Ft. Bragg told me that she saw a mandatory counselor after her tour in Afghanistan, who said that even though she "did not see combat" and was "mostly on base," she might have some reentry issues. He had no idea that she had served an eight-month tour as part of a special operations team of women and had been on night raids several times a week throughout her deployment.[7]

With this new type of war, the United States needs new strategies for our veterans. The Road Home Program and their Center for Veterans and Their Families provides timely and confidential support, counseling, and veteran health services to help veterans and their families understand, heal from, and cope with the invisible wounds of war.

Will Beiersdorf is executive director of the Road Home Program. He served in both the Navy Reserve and the Illinois Army National Guard. He served during Desert Storm and Operation Enduring Freedom at Guantanamo Bay, Cuba. Upon his return, he and his wife, Marybeth, formed an organization called Salute!, which has helped over two thousand veterans in a number of social and referral services.

"The whole 9/11 event changed everybody's lives and laid a new sense of trauma and anxiety in everybody. It changed us and raised the bar for all of us. When these men and women are deployed they are asked to do things in challenging situations. When I returned, I was trying to explain to people what Cuba was like and explain that there's a war going. I would say, 'Don't you understand there's a sense of urgency?' I got the sense that they weren't really on board."

Will goes on to describe how he learned that this war is different and why new strategies are needed to address these differences.

"When the conflicts started, I'll be honest, I didn't fully comprehend the transition challenges facing men and women who were coming back from Afghanistan or Iraq. I did start to see it when I saw them deployed once, then a second time, and even deployed a third time. That's when I started to see what was going on with these men and women and their families who directly and indirectly were being grinded up in these events that they continually went back to.

"I think that is the real challenge of this generation. In this global war of terror, you're fighting an enemy, you're fighting an ideology, you're fighting something that is invisible. They use tools to terrorize and damage us not just physically but mentally as well. That's why the Road Home Program's help with posttraumatic stress and traumatic brain injury is critical."

Former VA secretary Eric K. Shineski offers his perspective on the differences between service members of the past and today's fighting force: "What is different about this generation? We've asked them to do a lot more, in a smaller serving force, in some of the longest wars in our history," Multiple deployments have created what he calls "a compounding effect" to health problems and combat stress, with an unknown overall cost. "There's more work to be done in terms of research and understanding of what the full impact is going to be."[8]

Erin P. Finley, PhD, is a medical anthropologist whose research concentrates on PTSD in veterans and its impact upon family members. She conducts extensive research at the Veterans Evidenced-based Research Dissemination and Implementation Center (VERDICT).

> But no matter how frequent the news reports, the burden of these wars has not, thus far, been a shared one. They have been paid for by the American people as a whole, but they have been largely fought and sacrificed for by military families and communities, leaving too many of the rest of us able to ignore the daily cumulative consequences.
>
> For now, the image of the service member who is left physically or psychologically injured by war remains a powerful one in the American psyche. Despite the presence of considerable stigma around PTSD, I think most Americans in the abstract at least are sympathetic toward service members and their postwar remains, however, whether Americans will continue in the commitment to the finish, and when the health-care education and other resources required by veterans may begin to seem—as they have after prior wars—like too much of a burden.
>
> Veterans with PTSD can at times present as unsympathetic figures. As the perceived glory of their service fades into the past, it can become too easy to focus on the anger and aggression associated with their illness.[9]

Lack of sympathy can lead to tragic circumstances, as noted in this *Washington Post* article from 2014:

> Staff Sgt. Robert D. Carlson raised the gun to his head. In the parking lot of their duplex, his wife was calling the police. "Please help," she cried. "He punched me in the face." His intention, Carlson would say later, was to kill himself. Instead, alone on the second floor of their house, he lowered the gun from his head, pointed it toward a window and squeezed the trigger again and again, nine times in all.
>
> Some of the rounds went into the roof of a garage, just below the window. Two rounds hit apartment buildings across the street. One round flew into the headlamp of a responding police SUV. That was July 2012.
>
> Now, two years later, after being found guilty of assault with a deadly weapon and sentenced to eight years in prison, Carlson wonders about the fairness of such a punishment. "I know I did wrong," he said recently from the detention facility at Joint Base Lewis-McCord in Washington state.
>
> But is jail time appropriate for someone who, before he fired those shots, spent 16 months in Iraq, followed by 12 months in Iraq, followed by another 12 months in Afghanistan? Forty months' total at war: He had survived a blast from a suicide car bomb. He had killed an Iraqi insurgent as the man's children watched in horror. He had traded

places one day with a fellow soldier who then was killed by a sniper's bullet, standing in the very place where Carlson would have been if he hadn't switched. Did his years in combat mean he was deserving of compassion?[10]

Military life instills and fosters an individual's sense of purpose. Sgt. Carlson had this sense of purpose. So why do we bother getting out of bed in the morning? We do it because we have a sense of purpose, a need to fill. As I was leaving the service, for two years I asked myself, "What am I going to do now?" One of the saddest things I have experienced is watching my mother whose sense of purpose was gone when my father died. "What am I going to do now?" she would ask me, just like my veterans.

The easiest answer for the "What do I do now?" question for veterans is to find meaningful work. Veterans have a strong sense of purpose, engrained in them when they first joined the military. After all, they have given their country four, ten, twenty, thirty, and sometimes forty years of service. Upon discharge or retirement, many long to find ways to continue to serve. Some people think that all veterans want to do is hang around the VA or local hospital. The vast majority want to continue to serve.

The best way for veterans to continue to serve is to find meaningful work. But not just any work. While working for a warehouse or handing out carts at Walmart is perfectly fine, many veterans, particularly the younger ones, are most anxious to continue to serve in ways they are accustomed to.

Most veterans want more than just a paycheck; they want to continue to serve and build another career. Positive things begin to happen when people start feeling good about themselves.

7

CAREERS, NOT JOBS

I want to look back on my career and be proud of the work, and be proud that I tried everything.[1]

—Jon Stewart, *The Daily Show*

The EN-Abled Veteran Internship is both story and journey. It begins with Dr. Mark Pollack, the Grainger Professor of Psychiatry and chairperson of the Department of Psychiatry at Rush Medical College. Pollack received his MD in 1982 from New Jersey Medical School and completed residency and fellowship training in psychiatry at Massachusetts General Hospital where he served as director of the Center for Anxiety and Traumatic Stress Disorders and professor of psychiatry at Harvard Medical School until 2011, when he began his work at Rush University Medical Center. While in Boston, Dr. Pollack was part of the Home Base Program. The mission of Home Base, a Red Sox Foundation and Massachusetts General Hospital program, is to heal the invisible wounds for post-9/11 veterans, service members, and their families through world-class clinical care, wellness, education, and research.[2]

Dr. Pollack and I have developed a great partnership working on problems and solutions for veterans and information technology support for psychiatry. He reinforces to me the idea of building coalitions, something that would be a major challenge for the Road Home Program.

Shortly after his arrival in 2012, he asked for my help with soliciting donations from some of the larger information technology firms I had worked with. While I explained that it would be difficult to get donations from technology account managers, I asked if perhaps the Road Home Program was considering vocational training in addition to outreach and clinical support. While he said that Road Home was not going to pursue vocational training or rehabilitation, he was very supportive of the idea, but I would have to be the one to figure it out.

I did, and I called it the EN-Abled Veteran Internship.

I pitched the idea to Lac Tran, CIO, who, being a veteran himself, was very supportive. Lac, born in Viet Nam, was an American citizen trained as a helicopter pilot fighting with the United States against North Viet Nam. He reminded me of the budget constraints and I readily agreed that would be a challenge. I also pitched the idea to our chief operating officer, Bobby Clapp. Bobby had a son in the Naval Academy and he was all over this idea. We had known each other for about three years and I began to look at Bobby as a positive mentor.

My concept going in was to not charge the veterans for the internship and just have them volunteer, but Lac had another idea. "I like the tuition-free idea, but Jaime, we should give them something [in return]. Sometimes it's the littlest things that can make a difference in someone's life."

I agreed and we settled on a rate of $12.50/hr., two days a week for twenty-six weeks. It came out to a whopping $5,200 per veteran, which is probably less than the city, fed, and state pay veterans sitting at home watching television.

I always came away with incredible energy after speaking with Bobby and was pumped about working with him, seeking his guidance and wisdom. Unfortunately, Bobby died in September 2012 and didn't live to see our success. In 2015, I won the award named after him, the J. Robert Clapp Jr. Diversity Award, which was such an honor. I miss Bobby to this day and despite the internship's success, I often wonder what it might have become under his leadership.

I also have to give credit to the U.S. Air Force for giving me the tools to put the internship together with a clear structure and format. There is a reason that the Air Force motto is "Aim High," which is certainly what I did in developing the strategy and curriculum for the EN-Abled Veteran Internship. I had no idea how I could get this internship off the ground, especially since I had no staff, no budget, and no clear picture of what I wanted to accomplish—other than finding jobs for veterans.

Funny, but the Air Force has a way of teaching you things that, at the time, you feel are insignificant, incredibly boring, or of no value whatsoever. Well, of course, I was wrong then, but I think I got it right now.

To start, I knew I needed a mission statement, so I came up with this: "The EN-Abled Veteran Internship will provide the necessary online and on the job training, resume support and job interview skills to create a polished market ready professional ready to begin a successful career in healthcare information technology." Now I thought that sounded pretty good. It was simple, satisfied some type of need, all the while supporting a great cause. Logically, following a mission statement, one needs to have some internship objectives—as outlined below:

Recognizing the needs of returning military veterans and their families, the EN-Abled Veteran Internship has developed the following objectives to help.

- Develop skills to obtain a career in health IT through successful Epic certification and employment.
- Leverage partnerships with healthcare institutions, community colleges and our IT vendor community to create opportunities for veterans and their families to learn new IT skills that make them competitive and employable in three months or less.
- Be part of a focused leading-edge internship. With the nationwide shortage of qualified Electronic Medical Record (EMR) specialists, employee skills obtained through the internship will bridge the gap between military and civilian careers.
- Tell their story. Veterans will engage with employees, sharing their experiences and history and creating a greater understanding of life in the military and the sacrifices and services they made to preserve the freedoms we all enjoy.
- Reproduce this successful model for any organization willing to hire veterans and put them to work as IT professionals nationwide.

I liked this too, as it added a universal approach: other organizations could use this as a model to build their own internships. I didn't want the internship to be another staff augmentation internship. While such an approach is highly successful in recruiting talent, I wanted to build an internship that could be reproduced anywhere in the United States. In order to do this, the internship had to be simple, straightforward, and sellable to senior hospital executives whose buy-in would be crucial to success.

I decided to make some proclamations, some of which turned out to be flat-out mistakes. The first one was, "We will not hire vets from this internship," which would ensure its reproducibility.

The second proclamation was, "This will be a twenty-six-week internship that will allow veterans to go to school and take care of clinic appointments." After all, veterans have a lot going on and I didn't want to interfere with other activities in their lives.

The third and (thankfully) last proclamation was, "We will take all veterans, regardless of their situations, into this internship."

Such proclamations were very bad mistakes and needed to be modified. Here's why. Not hiring veterans to augment staff was a bad idea from the beginning. What flipped the switch here was one veteran who told me that he was being evicted, the repo man was lurking, and he had no other job prospects. The vet did well during a competitive interview, so the policy was changed to competitively hire veterans if job openings were available. Veterans had to apply and compete just like everyone else. We weren't offering charity, and the veterans certainly weren't asking for it anyway. The first pilot group in 2013, brave souls that they were, immediately railed against the idea of twenty-six weeks, as they said it was too long for them to give priority to the internship, and besides, they needed jobs now! So I switched it to four days per week for thirteen weeks, which accelerated learning and was cost neutral.

Accepting all veterans became unworkable. Since we partner with staffing firms for resume guidance and interview coaching, we were not doing anyone a favor, particularly veterans, by taking all applicants. Staffing firms put their reputations on the line, and if on intake we feel a veteran won't be hirable, why waste his or her time and dash their expectations? We have to be thinking of the end product in order to be successful with our partners.

Not all veterans belong in this internship. Some veterans have neither the desire nor the acumen to work with computers. Some veterans performed poorly and I had to come to grips with the fact that there was nothing I could do for them. This was probably the toughest lesson I had to learn. Try as I might, I couldn't save them all. And it wasn't my fault that I couldn't save them. Such survival has to come from the instinct of the veterans themselves, nowhere else. This was something that other veteran supporters already knew, but I had to learn it the hard way by seeing it for myself.

Undeterred, I remembered what Dr. Pollack told me about building a coalition. Since I had no budget, no staff, no classrooms, and no curriculum, I needed help. That coalition would have to involve internal, community, profit and not-for-profit sources, and maybe city, state, and federal involvement. Plus, my IT staff and myself already had day jobs.

I started by considering who within my sphere of influence would share the common passion of helping veterans. My first idea was to follow what Dr. Pollack had asked about: my vendor partner relationships. I believe that philanthropy is an art form, and I proved that it was not in my skill set to try and sell to my former military friends and associates. I have an appreciation for those who can do this, but I'm just not one of them.

I knew that I had to build a coalition. Some people say that I'm good at building coalitions, but not really. I just try to find those that share the same values and priorities that I have and try to put people together to meet shared goals. Many people want to help veterans and my job was to foster and advance that shared belief.

My first outreach was to Microsoft. Since we were an academic medical center and used an edu domain, the generous Microsoft IT Academy online training curriculum was made available to all EN-Abled Veterans in the internship. The academy offers training on the majority of its business and personal computing software programs, which could help veterans both professionally and personally.

So instead of asking corporations for money, I decided to ask for training.[3] In return, I got partners who might offer a training opportunity similar to Microsoft's, or provide access to training that was freely available to the general public. Either way, this type of exposure was a great adjunct to the on-the-job training that was the basis of the EN-Abled Vet Internship. Some companies had no online training, so my pitch was for these companies to go back and think of something else. They responded. For example, Trend Micro offered free antivirus cards. Many veterans were both thankful and confused. No one ever gave them this kind of gift without asking for anything in return. But it was free to them and they certainly appreciated the gift.

The next step was to develop some key performance indicators (KPIs). These would be used as guidelines and metrics necessary to ensure a successful training program.

- KPI #1: EN-Abled Veteran Internship gives veterans the opportunity for on-the-job training (OJT).

  EN-Abled Veteran Internship will help interns develop the workplace information technology skills in a hospital environment to help them achieve the opportunity for gainful employment.

  The EN-Abled Veteran Internship recognizes on-the-job training as a vital part to a veteran's potential for employment. Such training should consist of the following components:

  1. Adequate training must be available to give the veteran the practical information they need.
  2. Appropriate information technology staff will be available to mentor and shadow the veteran to facilitate knowledge and sharing of information with a subject matter expert.

3. Flexible scheduling to ensure time is available for the veteran to absorb the training material and the on-the-job training experience.

4. Creation of an engaging work center that encourages the veteran to be given a warm welcome and safe environment for acceptance, learning, growing, and enjoying the comradery and collaboration provided by the entire EN-Abled Veteran Internship experience.

- KPI #2: Classrooms without walls.

    The EN-Abled Veteran Internship will make available any and all current training materials associated with learning new skills or enhancing existing skills learned during military service.

    1. Encourage the veteran to explore online training that may be free or readily available at low cost.

    2. Veterans may not have computers or the high-speed internet access necessary for online training in their homes. Such tools will be necessary in order to maintain flexibility and connectivity. Loaner equipment will be distributed as needed.

    3. Partner with organizations that are supportive of veterans. Many academic and commercial schools and businesses offer coursework or training opportunities. Such opportunities or training may be available from prominent IT vendors or other organizations advancing veteran employment.

- KPI #3: Spouse and adult child employment.

    1. If the military veteran is ill for an extended period of time, EV may accept the spouse or adult dependent into the program.

    2. We recognize that household income shouldn't be a barrier to veteran recovery.

- KPI #4: Unique resume and job interviewing techniques.

    1. We bring in staffing firms that help with resume development. These consulting firms perform resume refresh and mock job interviews, as well as conduct job searches.

    2. While the services are pro bono, the consulting firm is not restricted from making a job placement and obtaining the appropriate finder's fee. Therefore, the consultants have a vested interest in veteran placement.

Tommy Bankhead is the manager for the EN-Abled Veteran Internship. He has been managing the customer service department for seven years. "I spent four years in the Navy where I served as a quartermaster on the ship the USS *Ferris*. When I got out in April of 1988, the benefits for Illinois veterans were pretty good, so I got four years of free college and an internship at Arthur Anderson.

"The transition that I had compared to the transition today, from what I hear from the veterans and from what I see, the transition is totally different. It was fairly simple, things like if you applied for the post office and police force, you got extra consideration on your application. But having said that, I didn't know that I was eligible for unemployment benefits."

Here is how he sees the EN-Abled Veteran Internship experience.

"We have a wide range of veterans that come to us with a wide range of skill sets and, along with that, some personal challenges. We worked through their technical skill and personalities and we've been able to work through a lot of them. I find that most people want to help veterans when they come here. The staff do get a little frustrated sometimes, but you can still see and feel that they genuinely want to help. Most of the veterans that come here want help. Some need a little more help than we can give them; they may not be ready to be in a work center just yet.

"Overall, the veterans seem genuinely happy when they come here. What I've seen is that when they come here, they are a totally different person after four weeks. A lot of it is because they gain confidence in demonstrating what they can do. You can see that because when we show them things and teach them, they want more. They perform the task and they become proud in their success, the ability to learn and apply a new skill that they didn't have coming in. They'll say, 'Oh yeah, I can do this!' Oftentimes, they just want to continue to do THAT and kind of stay in their lane, but we push them to learn more because there is so much to learn and we only have them for thirteen weeks. And overall, they pretty much step up. Except for a few, they all seem to really enjoy the internship. They promote the internship to other people outside and often try to get their friends to come and join the internship. When they first come here, their resume is often not well written. Their personal interview skills appear to be there. After working with our support staffing firms who help with polishing up their resumes, doing mock up job interviews, and building LinkedIn accounts, you can see the improvement in how they carry themselves in a much more positive way.

"The veterans start slow in developing relationships and interacting with staff, which is to be expected, especially since they are a little guarded about people in general. There are trust issues on both sides, really. But the fact that we have military on staff allows for greater integration into projects. We push them to give them a chance. In some cases, we need to take things a little slower. So sometimes we have to make some adjustments to give them more experience and feel more comfortable."

My advice for those that want to create their own EN-Abled Veteran Internship?

1. Be open minded. Don't close the door because of someone's personality or someone's language, or what someone looks like. A lot of people tend to see that immediately and that stops them from wanting to help.
2. Because they don't have the same level of skill or education you have, give them the opportunity to show what they can do. And then teach them.
3. Share with them what they are doing wrong and help them. Remember, many of these vets for years wore the same color pants and same color shirt. Help them make the right choices for clothing in the work environment. These seem like little things to us when they come in to the internship, but for veterans, they may not pick up on some of the subtleties of the civilian workplace.
4. You may have a plan as to how you want them to do things, but give them a chance to show you what they know. Let them show you what they got.
5. Don't treat them like veterans. Don't treat them like military. Let them know that they are now in the corporate world, and that these are how things happen in the corporate world.
6. They do need some flexibility, but keep it short. Otherwise, they get the wrong idea how the corporate world works.
7. Don't be afraid of making mistakes. The reason I told you the history of the EN-Abled Veteran Internship is to show you that I made plenty of mistakes. But I listened to my staff, I listened to my veterans, and I was not afraid to admit I was wrong. This process is an evolving one and as long as you have the support and resolve, you, too, will be successful.

This is an experience that I am so glad to be a part of. Yes, they have learned from me but I have also learned a lot from them and about myself. I have learned to be more patient and supportive of the veterans, and with members of my staff, as well. Having the veterans around has made me a better manager. Many of the vets in the internship have come to find themselves again.

As the "Chief Dreaming Officer" of this internship, I make it a point never to ask veterans probing questions about their military experience or personal lives. It's my turn to don't ask, don't tell. I do this for several reasons: it's none of my business, it's illegal, it's intimidating to them, and besides, I don't really care to know. For if I do, it may influence how veterans do in the internship. Once they get with the team and feel comfortable, then many will start opening up. But they don't really disclose anything to me unless they want to or they have agreed to be interviewed.

In our internship, a veteran can go through the entire thirteen weeks or longer and I might never know what medical condition, if any, they have. I did have one veteran come in and we compared our Walgreen deep-dish pill containers, but that's about it. During the four years of this internship, we have witnessed a veteran

- Experience a five-day blackout due to a medication error, followed by a two-week inpatient medication baseline stay (we're still not sure he ever found his car).
- Forget the month/day/year.
- Wear the same hoodie and jeans every day (we found out later that he was homeless).
- Insist that he had to wear a three-piece suit, despite the fact that he was crawling under tables for eight hours a day.
- Go through a transgender process.
- Flash back and run out when he saw a hijab.
- Tell stories that the FBI was watching him because his brother was a fugitive and on their Ten Most Wanted List.

We took on all types of qualified veterans with all types of conditions, known or unknown. We created a diverse population of veterans who inspired themselves, their fellow veterans, and the permanent staff that was training them. Not everybody was successful, but despite their disabilities or age, we took a chance on them when nobody else would. Later on, you will learn how you can do the same. I learned that when an encouraging and accepting work environment is created, anything can happen.

8

AT THE INTERSECTION OF HUMAN SPIRIT AND THEOLOGY

We have just enough religion to make us hate, but not enough to make us love one another.[1]

—Jonathan Swift, Anglo Irish satirist

What happens in the battle when humanity and religion come together? I think it's safe to say, "just about anything." My first instinct was to say "conflict." But building a caring and nurturing work environment has another answer.

"My name is Ryan Russell and I am a marine. I was born in Kenosha, Wisconsin, and lived most of my life in Silver Lake. I lived there until I was nineteen. I only joined the Marine Corps because I didn't want to go to college because part of me doesn't like the idea of school because a lot of schools aren't testing for knowledge, they're testing for test taking skills. I thought the next best thing was the Marines and I thought, 'Well, if I'm going to go do this, I'm going to go hard.'

"I enlisted in the Marine Corps and, man, that completely threw my life into an upside-down whirlwind. It was really tough. The thing about it is you're going to make it if you just don't quit. Drill instructors are not going to make it so that you can't make it. You're gonna get past everything. You just have to learn how to push yourself.

"Boot camp is learning how to push yourself knowing that you can go further. When you're in boot camp, you're too scared to cry, thinking that your drill instructor is going to find you and see you crying and you don't know what is going to happen after that.

"In the Marines, I was a 3131 Operator. I drove big, giant trucks. It was fun. I liked it. I ended up serving in the Marine Corps for three years and three months.

"One day, I was out on my motorcycle and had an accident. I was in a coma for eleven days and I had gotten a traumatic brain injury (TBI), which means that I cut my brain really bad. I would explain the accident, only thing is, I don't remember it. I hit the ground pretty hard. It happened on a Friday and the only thing I can remember is the previous Tuesday.

"My helmet was found thirty feet from me. It was a $900 helmet and it sucked because I was in the hospital for six months because of this, just to recover and learn how to do everything again. I remember that I had to learn my name again, interesting fact to know. When I did get my helmet back from storage, it was completely destroyed. I couldn't even look at it. It was weird. I had to have another Marine take it out of my sight because I couldn't stand to look at it. But I still wear my boots—all the time.

"The accident happened on October 17, 2014, and I was discharged October 30, 2015. I don't know how it took them a year, but I was still on active duty getting paid, which was nice.

"I don't have a lot of memories about the accident but I do have this memory of pain. I don't know what it was or what was going on. I know that I will never recover from my TBI. It gets better all the time, but I'm going to have problems with it for the rest of life. It's just a fact I gotta deal with.

"The VA was still following me, but it was so overwhelming because I had so much to do. I won't blame it on them, but I will blame a lot of it on myself. It just sucked and it was an overflow of everything. I think it was because of my TBI and I had to get checked up on everything. My social worker helped me through that.

"We had a talk with my parents, asking me why I'm missing so many appointments and stuff. It was just too much and [my social worker] reduced my number of appointments from six per week down to one per week. I still see my VA social worker today. She's awesome and she has helped me through a lot of things.

"I was home for a little while, but I eventually got a job working for a retail technology company. I worked there for about eight months, but they had problems with me learning. They weren't on me or reinforcing. I have problems remembering things. They didn't like that I have to write down everything that I had to know and then go home and study it so that I could be ready for the next day. Keep repeating it.

"They didn't like the way I treated some of the other employees. You see, the Marine Corps really did change me like it did every other Marine that goes through it. I was just really rough on everyone [*laughs*]. Just do the job, don't complain, just do it. There's nothing to complain about. Like, you're getting paid, you're here, it's your option.

"You know, we have it insanely nice here. I think it's crazy 'cause, uh, I hear people complain about their cars sometimes, like I don't like this one; I want a new one. You're lucky you have a car!

"I then went to work at a large warehouse. It was horrible. I was a storer, standing in one spot, just scanning items into a bin ten hours a day. I hated it and walked off the job. No one was happy there.

"So I went jobless for a while. It was rough. I would apply to places and get turned down, either through a phone call or email. That was weird because I thought a lot of people would want to hire a Marine, that's what I thought when I got out, but it's not too common, honestly.

"I think there is a stigma with the military, especially the Marines, sometimes with PTSD. A lot of people think that is going to be a 'thing.' Filling out applications, I know I don't have to, but I do disclose that I am a disabled veteran and I do believe that was a significant factor as to why I was not being hired.

"Through my social worker, I was connected to Dee Barnes at the Veterans Rehabilitation Unit (VRU) at Naval Station Great Lakes in North Chicago, Illinois. She drove me in and introduced me and I just loved it. I started the program a week or two later and I've loved it ever since.

"I started by working in the Audio-Visual Department and was dressed nicely. I was working with the staff who told me to cool it down dress-wise. I can do that. The experience was pretty awesome. I will say it was a little overwhelming with all the stuff I had to learn, but the staff was awesome and everybody there was dedicated to helping me. They all cared about the vet, which is awesome, because I have seen that a lot of people just don't care about us, for some reason.

"Things were not working out the best for me, so I got transferred to the end user technology team. For the first couple of weeks, it was opening boxes and getting product ready. I loved it because I love hands-on work, which is consistent with the lifestyle of my family.

"Moving to this new team had a huge impact on me because everybody knows I don't remember everything. I don't forget everything but there are a lot of things I do forget. For me to remember, it just has to be repeated and repeated and repeated and it's awesome being in the technology expansion room with Karim, and he knows I need things to be repeated. He didn't have a problem with it, he just kept on repeating and repeating. He's dedicated to helping me learn.

"Everybody here is so much more accepting and everyone here is respectful, which is nice. The jobs at other places that I worked at didn't work out. Other employees thought that I didn't know nothing or that I can't remember things, it was just horrible.

"It's nice at EN-Abled Vet because they know you have problems, yet they are going to respect you and treat you the same as everyone else. . . . Everyone is so nice, so accepting, it's awesome. Most definitely, this program has therapeutic qualities. It made me feel like I'm accepted back into society and it has definitely helped me back to regular society life. In my other jobs, like I said, all I knew was to go hard and rough on people, which is what the Marine Corps put into me. I'm not saying it's a bad thing, but it's not a good thing for everyone.

"After the accident and when I was discharged, the Marine Corps was all that I really knew. I didn't know who I was for a long time, I just knew who the Marine Corps thought I was and I was that person. So being rough on everyone was all that I knew. But at EN-Abled Vet, I learned how to be nice, which is cool. I now have huge self-esteem. I didn't think it's a big thing, but others do. I take a two-hour train ride to get here and two hours back. I don't mind waiting because in the military you get used to waiting.

"I like to show up to places a half-hour early, which is something I'm used to but drives my friends crazy. On the train ride, I just get more sleep. I work very hard at work trying to remember things and am very tired at the end of the day. I make dinner and go right to sleep. And repeat.

"So now I'm ready for the next part of my life. I got a letter recently from the Department of Veterans Affairs, and I went, 'oh man.' I was worried because every time I had gotten a letter from them, it was something I needed to worry about or something extremely bad. But this letter was different for me. It was talking to me about the post-9/11 GI Bill and told me that I was verifiable at 100 percent. My tuition is paid for, my housing is covered for up to $1200/month . . . free school, that's insane! I plan to go to University of Wisconsin–Madison. I'm extremely excited."

Abdelkrim (Karim) Belkhos is the employee cited by Ryan Russell as being instrumental in his success in the EN-Abled Vet Internship Program. Born in Algeria and of French descent, Karim moved to the United States a few decades ago to build a new life for himself and his family. A man of strong Muslim faith, Karim is an outstanding employee.

Karim cares deeply about patient care and anyone else fortunate to be along his path. His heart is an open book when it comes to sharing his love of people and his love of helping others less fortunate. He shares what it was like to work in the EN-Abled Vet program, particularly with Ryan.

"My name is Karim and I have been working at the hospital [Rush] for eight years on the PC [patient care] refresh team. I do the best I can for this hospital to save lives and I try to do the best I can to make this the best hospital.

"I appreciate that veterans are brought into the program. When they come, the first thing I do is show them hospitality and a warm welcome. I make sure that they see that we are people like them and when we show them that they are very welcome, they gain confidence. They become people that are willing to learn and are in the best position to get jobs.

"First thing we have to do with the veterans is to accept them. The first few days are hard, but after a while, when we know each other's character and attitude, we can teach them how to do things with the computer. When they are willing to learn and they are OK, we give them a process to follow. Some learn in a short period, some take a little longer. We teach them to image a computer, sometimes they forget, but after one to two weeks they are good. We encourage them to learn things and go home at night where they continue to learn.

"The most important thing is that we have to be patient. And we learn from them how to treat people. It's not just for them, but we learn, too. Sometimes we get really busy, but we work out a schedule for them. Even those that come from the battlefield; we have to treat them the same as other people. We can't see them as coming from a war. If we treat them like they are crazy people, it won't work.

"One vet, 'Bea,' was getting really frustrated. I took her away from the group and offered patience and kindness to help her through it. One day, she asked if she could play music that she liked and I said sure. It's your music, just don't play it too loud. And it was good. It was good music.

"I am Muslim and I like to help people. After Bea left, she could do everything we taught her on how to work with computers. Bea asked if she could come visit me and my family in Algeria and I said, 'Sure. You can come anytime and bring the whole family.'

"In my opinion, this EN-Abled Vet internship is very, very good. People just have to know and have to recognize that these are normal people like the rest of us. When they come, they are usually frustrated. They look at us differently. The vets have to learn and know things and make progress.

"They see us working and that we are very busy, and their reaction is, 'Oh, I am not from this world.' Step by step, smiling, I ask, 'Can you share some gum with me?' 'I have a piece of candy.' 'How about some food?' It seems small, but it means a lot to build this connection and makes them not afraid to talk to me.

"You see what their skills are and you find out how they work. Then you learn at different levels. Give each one a time to learn. Then you separate them from each other in the workplace. Most important is patience and treating them like a human being. It doesn't matter who they are, black, white race, religion, Asian people. I meet the Jewish people, Sid. I am Muslim. I treat him very well. As he was leaving me, we were hugging, Jewish and Muslim.

"Ryan was the best [*big smile*]. It was like losing a son to me when he left. He was so young and, I don't know, it was like he wanted to learn and be in this world. He had his own family, but I hosted him like a son. I would say, 'Son, are you coming today?' Sometimes he would not come in and I would call him and he would tell me that he forgot it was a workday. No big deal, come in tomorrow.

"I taught Ryan how to image computers, join them to the domain. After three to four weeks, I gave him twenty computers; there were no mistakes. He was helped by another vet, too, who was more advanced.

"I thought it was better for him to stay with me. When he left, he and me we were both heartbroken. With patience and respect, I brought him from a bad world to real life; it's like virtual to real life. That is the purpose of what I do.

"It's a very good experience; I wish we could get a lot more people. Ryan left me too early. He is going to school now and it is going to work. I have 100 percent confidence in my son. He will push himself from the inside.

"If you put my name in your book, if I go to anywhere in the world. I will not be scared. I am providing relief for military people. And if I am a Muslim, in the ocean, in a sinking boat and I see Jewish people around, I will ask for their help. If I don't ask for help, I'm going to die. It's suicide. It's a hellfire for my belief. If you bring me people, I don't see the other side. They come, I am Muslim, they need my help, I will help. I will give them everything, time, knowledge, whatever.

"I do not say these things because I want to show that I am the best. Ryan, for me, was like a son. When I lost him, when he left, I was heartbroken. He was my son. He is moving far away from me. I have children that are Ryan's age. At work, we are like a small family, brother, sister, father, son. The only thing I am disappointed with is losing Ryan. He left me too soon. I lost my son."

9

REMEMBERING EQUALITY
IN THE WORKPLACE

My role was to bring about fairness in the workplace. All I did was implement the laws that were currently on the books.[1]

—Hilda Solis, U.S. Secretary of Labor, 2009–2013

The Rehabilitation Act of 1973, as amended in 1992 and 1998, and the Rehabilitation Act of 1990 are corollary pieces of civil rights legislation that created civil rights laws enforcing equal opportunity and protecting individuals with disabilities from discrimination. The Rehabilitation Act provides for direct services to individuals with the goal of providing skills and training to help individuals with disabilities become qualified for employment. It is important for all organizations to be familiar with the Rehabilitation Act and its amendment as well as the Americans with Disabilities Act (ADA) of 1992.

Deborah Leuchovius is an ADA specialist at the PACER Center. She provides an overview of these important acts:

Knowledge of how the two laws work together—where one leaves off and another steps in—can help individuals with disabilities prepare for success in the work force and advocate for their rights in society.

Each law has had an influence on the other. The ADA was influenced by the earlier Rehabilitation Act in several important ways. First, Congress was convinced that the Rehabilitation Act alone was not sufficient to end the widespread discrimination against people with disabilities that exists in this country. Secondly, where courts interpreted the Section 504 antidiscrimination provisions very narrowly, Congress clarified their intention to provide broader protections in the ADA. Finally, much of the ADA is based on Section 504 of the Rehabilitation Act and its regulations.

In turn, the ADA influenced the Rehabilitation Act during its reauthorization in 1992. In 1992, the Rehabilitation Act was amended to reflect the language, goals and objectives of the ADA. The Rehab Act adopted the ADA's emphasis on integration as its own, and translated the principles and policies of the ADA into government rehabilitation programs for people with disabilities.

Of critical importance is the assumption that people with disabilities—including individuals with the most severe disabilities—can work. This is important because prior to the ADA, government agencies providing rehabilitative services assumed that most people with severe disabilities were not employable. Now they must assume that individuals with even the most severe difficulties can work, and the burden lies with the state rehabilitation program to prove that they cannot.

The integration of people with disabilities into the mainstream of society is also fundamental to both laws. Separate settings or programs are not acceptable unless necessary to ensure equal benefit.[2]

Specifically, ADA is a civil rights law that prohibits discrimination against an individual with a disability. Among its many provisions and benefits, the ADA requires employers to provide "reasonable accommodations" to their employees with disabilities, empowering them to have the same rights and privileges as all others in the workplace environment. Reasonable accommodation includes such things as equal access, adaptive technology, flexible schedules, and modified job descriptions. Such provisions give equal opportunity to achieve the important things in life inside and outside of work.

In a letter to White House dated July 26, 2007, the National Council on Disability (NCD) describes the impact of the ADA and progress toward achieving its goals.

The provisions of the ADA addressing architectural, transportation, and communication accessibility have changed the face of American society in numerous concrete ways, enhancing the independence, full participation, inclusion, and equality of opportunity for Americans with disabilities. Americans with disabilities report having greater access to goods and services from businesses, state and local governments, and their local communities. People with mobility impairments have experienced substantial improvements in physical access to transportation, businesses and government agencies. As workers, people with disabilities are more likely to receive accommodations and less likely to be terminated due to their disabilities. However, obtaining employment remains difficult for people with visible and severe disabilities. Disparities still exist in access

to health insurance, health care, and financial assets for people with disabilities, as compared to people without disabilities. Access to information, particularly the Internet, is inconsistent, at best, for people who are
visually impaired. Progress toward the goal of economic self-sufficiency
appears to be the goal having the least success.

The ADA impact report contains recommendations for addressing the
barriers that are preventing full achievement of the overarching goals of
the ADA, and NCD remains committed to working with the Administration, Congress, and the public to achieve the promise of the ADA
for all Americans—the elimination of disability-based discrimination in
all aspects of society.[3]

Here is one example of how important it is to understand these laws
and how adequate training and documentation must be in place in order to
ensure the elements of the laws are understood and followed.

One day, open-door policy fully intact, Dwaine came into my office
waving a piece of paper above his head.

"Sir, we are at war! This is it! I am going to contact the head of the
VA, I'm going to file an EOE [Equal Opportunity Employer] complaint, I
am getting a lawyer and you're not going to get away with this. I am the
victim of a great injustice and if you or anybody else think they are going
to get away with this, well, they don't know who they're up against, sir."

Twice a week Dwaine would come into my office with the latest
news headlines telling me to grab my duffel bag because he and I were
going back to fight. Tongue in cheek, of course, but a great conversation
nonetheless. I was in my mid to late fifties, never deployed to a warzone,
and certainly did not want to go back nor go over for the first time, not
now with my aches and pains.

But this energy from Dwaine was different. He was mad, not excited.

"Calm down, Dwaine. Hold on a minute. Have a seat and let me
see if I can understand what is going on. This has got to be some type of
misunderstanding and I'm sure we can work this out," I said. But Dwaine
was just getting started.

"This is the end. I've seen this thing before. They're trying to get rid
of me, sir. I know how the paper trail works and if you think I'm going
to take this, well, I tell you what, sir, I'm coming back at ya. I know my
rights and this place is going down."

"OK, OK, OK, Dwaine. Have a seat and help me understand what it
is that has gotten you so angry."

"Sir, you know I am 100 percent service connected disabled. Everybody knows this. For them to start this type of discipline and start to

throw me out of this place is wrong and I'll be damned if I am going to go through this shit, sir."

"Dwaine, let me look at this document," I replied. By now the document was crinkled and well-worn as he handed it over to me. Turns out, this was a human resources standard form, given to employees to document minor infractions and corrective action. It was a Level One disciplinary document designed to point out a minor incident, to document that incident and present the form to the employee for review and signature. Such a signature does not admit blame; it simply means that the document had been presented to the employee. The employee can choose to sign it or leave the signature block blank. Predictably, Dwaine did not sign because he believed this to be an admission of guilt that would be used against him in future.

Like other engineers, Dwaine was expected to pull call, which means that you will be available by phone to troubleshoot a problem or come into the medical center, as necessary. Two nights prior, Dwaine was paged and did not respond. Failure to respond can lead to delay in addressing a serious incident within information systems and/or the medical center that could potentially have a direct impact to patient care. When Dwaine failed to respond, his managers followed the usual disciplinary action, which, in this case, was the Level One disciplinary action.

In Dwaine's Army world, such documents can be used to trigger a formal military dismissal process, which can be started by a small infraction. Such documents can be used in yearly enlistment evaluations and has the potential to derail a career, particularly at the senior enlisted level. Since this is the process Dwaine is most familiar with, and knowing that this is his default knee-jerk reaction, he believed we were presenting this document in an effort to build a case to get rid of him.

"Listen to me, Dwaine," I said. "This document is not like an Army document and does not represent the same disciplinary escalation process you may be familiar with. In the civilian world, this process is basically a wakeup call designed to get the employee's attention. It usually is a one-time incident that does not necessarily lead to further disciplinary action nor career derailment."

But Dwaine does not know this. He's never had to, until now.

"Sir, I don't care. I do not deserve this. You all know that when I take my sleeping pill I am out and nothing can wake me. You knew about this and I am not taking this lying down, sir."

"Tell you what, Dwaine," I said. "Under the Americans with Disabilities Act, an employer has the responsibility to provide 'reasonable accommodations' for employees who have disclosed and documented their disability or disabilities. In my opinion, exempting you from the call schedule is a fair and reasonable accommodation for you. This document is ill-advised and is not consistent with employee civil rights under the ADA. Does this approach seem right to you?"

"Well, sir, I feel a little bit better but something needs to be done so that this type of thing doesn't happen again. *That* will make me feel better."

"Understood, Dwaine. I will speak to your managers to educate them about the ADA and how we can create an environment to provide for such reasonable accommodations within the Information Systems Department. Having said all this, do you still want to pursue taking this matter up the chain of command?"

"No, sir," he responded. "I'm OK now, and I'm going back to work."

"Carry on, Sergeant," I said.

I took a deep breath and had a moment of reflection on something that I already knew to be true. Despite the advances and success gained from the ADA, the spirit and intent of the act was something that was not in the American psyche. Gaps still exist. Education and training is not being provided to the majority of business leaders. Which begs the question, Is the ADA working?

While challenges remain twenty-seven years after the ADA was signed into law, the law has improved aspects of daily life for many people with disabilities. The following account from the *Duluth News Tribune* in Minnesota takes a look at how far we have come from the passage of ADA, and how far we still have to go.

[Musician Gaelynn Lea Tressler], who uses a wheelchair, works as a fiddle instructor and regularly performs in the Twin Ports area. She hates being carried on stage, she said; it's something performers without disabilities don't have to deal with. . . . Tressler said that the law is "making it a little bit more acceptable in society so people are more used to seeing people's disabilities," . . . noting that people with disabilities were hidden from society not long ago. . . .

"What's the difference between a sign saying, 'You can't come in here,' or an actual barrier, an actual wall that you can't climb?" said John Nousaine, director of North Country Independent Living in Superior, an agency that provides programs and services to people with disabilities in Northwestern Wisconsin. . . .

"Most of the discrimination people have faced has been due to attitude and misconceptions about disability," he said. "I think the biggest thing now that is changing is—it's slow—but people are recognizing disability as just a naturally occurring thing."[4]

As promised, later on that day, I called Dwaine's manager and director into my office. "I spoke to Dwaine earlier today and he was pretty upset about getting a Level One this morning. Tell me what happened."

"Well," Dwaine's director replied, "Dwaine was on call and he never showed up. He didn't even call in or anything. So we gave him a Level One Disciplinary Incident Record."

"Guys, you can't do that," I explained. "Here's why. When Dwaine was hired, he provided full disclosure on his application. We have knowledge that Dwaine has a disability. There is something called the Americans with Disabilities Act which directs us to provide 'reasonable accommodations' for Dwaine because of his disability. To me, a reasonable accommodation would be for him not to pull call."

"But that's not fair," the manager replied. "Part of the duties of working here are to pull call and it's not fair to the others that Dwaine gets to be off the call schedule. This is really going to hurt morale if we have to make an exception for Dwaine."

From past experience, I knew that education and sensitivity were the order of the day. I kept my voice calm but leaned ever so slightly closer to my younger and less experienced director and middle manager.

"Look, you may think it's unfair and other staff members may feel the same way. But in my opinion, a fair and reasonable accommodation for this employee is to pull him off the call schedule. You and I both know his work ethic and his lifestyle and we hired him anyway. You also know that once he takes that sleeping pill, he is gone to the world until the next morning.

"The medications he is taking is helping him with his PTSD. Heck, the guy came into my office and told me his pharmaceutical ingestion timeline, as well as the added twelve-pack for a chaser. Given all the junk he is taking, I don't know how he can even walk. But he has a disability, we have knowledge, and it is our obligation to give employees like Dwaine these types of exceptions."

"I don't know, boss," was the reply. "Where is his Level One form now?"

"I tore it up and sent him back to work," I said.

"You did what? What did you do that for, Jaime?"

"The paper was useless and inappropriate for this situation," I replied. "Look, if we were to follow this course of disciplinary action, despite his hyperbole, we are sitting ducks to any type of agency Dwaine chooses to contact. I cannot say with a clear conscience that taking Dwaine off the call schedule is not a reasonable accommodation for Dwaine's disability. Guys, we lose this case every time. Try to reflect on what I'm telling you, then take Dwaine off the call schedule."

I realized just how close a call this was. If I wasn't educated and experienced with these matters, I probably would have told Dwaine to get out of my office and let the Level One stand. But because I was sensitized to these issues, I knew better. The average executive might not know, let alone appreciate, the rights of the disabled.

Arguing and judgment are counterintuitive to ADA and twenty-five years later, I am still convinced that employers need to have a human resources staff that incorporates disability awareness in the workplace. Larger businesses need ancillary staff to address needs, whether they are veterans or not. It doesn't matter.

Huge props to former president George H. W. Bush and to those who fight for equal rights for all. A lot of great work was done to get ADA in place and results show the progress this effort has made to date.

But the fight remains. The Dwaines of the world are assets to any organization for who they are and what they can do. They magnify the power of diversity. In the hiring process, it's not just the right thing to do, it's the law of the land. Organizations need to know this law and provide opportunities for the civil rights of the disabled, including military veterans. Organizations need to keep diversity front and center, not a rest stop on the highway and certainly not simply given lip service.

When you open your mind to new opportunities and new ways of doing things, amazing things happen.

10

NEW CLINICAL THERAPIES FOR
NEW TYPES OF WAR INJURIES

*When people call asking for PTSD treatment, half don't show up to
the first visit. It's hard to talk about. If we can find a way to make
treatment less awful and more humane, I'm all for it.*[1]

—Monnica Williams, professor of psychology,
University of Connecticut

Psychiatrists' management of shell shock, now referred to as PTSD, was
first recognized in World War I. Treatments were primitive, surgical,
or nonexistent. Men who isolated themselves from family and friends felt
that they just had to "suck it up." They suffered in silence, stuck in a morass
of pride and misunderstanding. Such was the zeitgeist of the soldier's life
post–World War I.

Medicine has come a long way since then, learning from mistakes of
the past and applying new technologies and treatment methodologies for
those with invisible wounds. Masic et al. describe a more modern approach
for those suffering invisible wounds.

> Evidence based medicine (EBM) is the conscientious, explicit, judicious
> and reasonable use of modern, best evidence in making decisions about
> the care of individual patients. EBM integrates clinical experience and
> patient values with the best available research information. It is a move-
> ment which aims to increase the use of high quality clinical research in
> clinical decision making. EBM requires new skills of the clinician, in-
> cluding efficient literature-searching, and the application of formal rules
> of evidence in evaluating the clinical literature.[2]

Basically, evidence based medicine addresses the following:

1. *The number of research studies* conducted that test the new treatment: one study isn't enough to really know whether or not a treatment works.
2. *The quality of those studies*: confidence and assurance grow when a study's findings are reproducible.
3. *Whether or not experts agree that the treatment works:* usually accomplished by top experts in the field that review the study and publish the findings in a prestigious medical journal.

Evidence based medicine is a powerful process in treating patients with PTSD. For example, early psychological interventions, including debriefing, were initially seen as promising therapy, but many of these interventions have now been disproved owing to a lack of evidence.[3]

There is strong evidence in the medical literature about the effectiveness of exposure therapy for PTSD patients. In a 2010 issue of *Annals of the New York Academy of Sciences*, "Psychiatry and Neurological Aspects of War," authors Judith Cukor et al. write about breakthrough evidence based treatments for PTSD. I've included their findings for a new treatment called exposure therapy:

> The evidence base for the treatment of PTSD offers effective options in the form of exposure therapies. Novel treatments, including couples and interpersonal therapies, virtual reality therapy, and the use of prazosin and DCS,[4] are being developed and evaluated through outcome trials.
>
> Yet, the task before us remains great. Chronic PTSD exists in large numbers throughout the world and especially among those sent to battle to protect our national interests. Our responsibility lies in the further development of alternative treatments and the dissemination of current evidence-based practices.
>
> Failure of providers to use established treatments is a barrier to effective care that as a community must be addressed. Controlled trials of new therapies need to be conducted before they can be added to the list of tools at the disposal of a clinician. Close examination of applications of current protocols to special populations may yield the development of modified treatments that can increase efficacy. While translational research stands to provide exciting contributions to our knowledge base, it must then be applied clinically to the implementation of differential therapeutics.
>
> In conclusion, exposure therapy is a powerful tool in the treatment of PTSD, and novel treatments are filling in the gap left by treatment failures. It remains incumbent upon the scientific community to put

evidence-based treatments in the hands of the clinicians and to develop and evaluate broader treatment options.[5]

Exposure therapy, as well as other evidence based practice (EBP) methods, is a major part of treatment at the Road Home Program. Since its inception in 2014, over two hundred veterans and their families have benefitted from the Road Home Program services, including support for TBI, PTSD, MST, combat operational stress reaction (COSR), and the social needs of the families of military veterans. All services are provided regardless of the veteran's ability to pay.

The Road Home Program does not compete with VA for services, rather it partners with the VA and similar organizations to expand outreach. Of particular importance is veterans' families, who are brought in as part of an overall comprehensive support system. In addition to the VA, the Road Home Program has built strong relationships with many Chicagoland-area veterans support organizations. The result is a strong cohesive network that supports each other and, more important, the veterans.

In 2015, the Road Home Program joined Emory Healthcare and Massachusetts General Hospital in creating a partnership with the Warrior Care Network. The mission of the Warrior Care Network, part of the Wounded Warrior Project, is to create a nationwide, comprehensive care network that will enhance access to the latest evidence based practices and expand services to include the needs of spouses and family members. Coordinated research, collaboration, and other types of information sharing enables this network to be a powerful force in major metropolitan areas with a high population of veterans and their families.[6]

The Road Home Program incorporates three identified therapies during treatment for PTSD.

Cognitive behavior therapy (CBT) is generally short term and focuses on helping clients deal with a very specific problem. During the course of treatment, people learn how to identify and change destructive or disturbing thought patterns that have a negative influence on behavior and emotions. The goal of CBT therapy is to teach veterans that while it is impossible to control the world or the surprises it brings, the veterans can control their reactions to events and stressors.

Exposure therapy is a technique in behavior therapy used to treat PTSD in a different way. Instead of pushing the traumatic event in the background, therapists reintroduce the event or image in an environment without danger. The veterans face their dreams and flashbacks head on. Numerous studies support this relatively new treatment for PTSD.

Counselling for families. Road Home recognizes the importance of family involvement in treating veterans. Family support is crucial to recovery. Will Beiersdorf described his experiences after he returned from service. He found it difficult to explain his sense of urgency to people back home. Even Chris Miller, who was separated from his unit for the last six months of his enlistment, experienced anxiety about relating to family and friends and being without his former unit.

According to writer David Wood, "moral injuries aren't always evident. But they can be painful and enduring." Woods wrote a series of articles for *Huffington Post* where he interviewed servicemen and women about their experiences:

> "Everybody has demons, but there are some wild kind of demons when you come back from combat," said a Navy corpsman (the Navy's name for its medics) who served a tour each in Iraq and Afghanistan and asked not to be identified by name. He was once unable to save a Marine with a terrible head wound, and afterwards felt other Marines blamed him. "You come home and ask yourself, what the hell did I do all that for? You gotta live with that shit and there's no program that the military can send you to or any class that's really gonna help."
>
> "Guilt is the root of it," he said. "Asking yourself, why are you such a bad person?" He wasn't that way before his military service. "I have a hard time dealing with the fact that I'm not me anymore. . . ."
>
> "People try to make sense of what happened, but it often gets reduced to, 'It was my fault,' 'the world is dangerous,' or, in severe cases, 'I'm a monster,'" explained Peter Yeomans, a staff psychologist at the VA Medical Center in Philadelphia. Many of his patients suffer from both Post Traumatic Stress Disorder and moral injury, and he is searching for ways to ease their pain. . . .
>
> For most veterans with moral injury, there is little help. In contrast to the extensive training and preparation the government provides troops for battle, the Defense Department and the VA have almost nothing specifically for the moral wounds that endure after they return. . . .
>
> The therapies and drugs developed to treat PTSD don't get at the root of moral injury, experts say, because they focus on extinguishing fear. PTSD therapy often takes the form of asking the patient to re-live the damaging experience over and over, until the fear subsides. But for a medic, say, whose pain comes not from fear but from losing a patient, being forced to repeatedly recall that experience only drives the pain deeper, therapists have found.
>
> "Medication doesn't fix this stuff," said Army psychologist John Rigg, who sees returning combat troops at Fort Gordon, Ga. Instead,

therapists focus on helping morally injured patients accept that wrong was done, but that it need not define their lives. . . . But by and large, those with moral injury are on their own.[7]

Michael B. Brennan is the associate clinical director of the Intensive Outpatient Program for the Road Home Program. I asked Dr. Brennan to describe what challenges veterans who come to the Road Home Program have and how evidence based practice plays a role in their recovery

"First, there's the stigma associated with asking for help. Veterans feel that they may not need help. They may be suspicious of the VA or other agencies based on stories they've read or the experiences of other war buddies. Other veterans are in such a dark place that they are unable to function due to their invisible wounds of war. They are in such a dark place that they are actually unable to believe what has happened to them, let alone express their feelings about it. Truth is, the military veteran comes home with an entirely different set of beliefs as a result of the high tension and operational stress faced on the battlefield.

"In order to recover, the veteran has to understand that during treatment things may get worse before they get better. Many of them face a pendulum situation. Some veterans have told me that they were a good person before they deployed, and a monster when they came back. 'People may treat me like a hero, but inside I feel like a baby killer. But I went overseas and had a job to do, and I did it. And by the way, why am I still alive, and is life worth living? Can you just make the pain to go away?'

"Their brains are going through what we call a contextual shift. Veterans are forced to retrain their brains and focus on daily living that doesn't involve the possibility of sudden death. A trip to the grocery store can help retrain the brain into realizing that routine trips are safe. Done on a repetitive scale, the brain retrains itself and puts more weight to life at home rather than life in a hostile environment.

"Our initial approach is to calm and reassure them that they are in a safe, nonjudgmental environment. To do that, about a third of our support staff are veterans themselves. We try to make a connection and build a sense of trust and from that trust, hopefully, an opening where we can provide tools and strategies that help the natural process of brain recovery and retraining.

"A lot of our success depends upon the veterans' motivation. You have to let the system work. The veteran has to allow us to help as we may have to go to several sources of pain to provide treatment. Trust and a safe haven are key steps to this healing process."

Dr. Niranjan Karnik, MD, PhD, is the medical director at the Road Home Program.

"At the Road Home Program, I see a generation of my age or younger who have had to go through a whole new set of wars that this country never planned for nor anticipated. Other wars had more defined outlines, what the signs were, what you are fighting for. It's so much more diffuse than it used to be and a lot of people are wondering what it is, what we're after, and what are we doing. It feels a lot less certain and the nature of war has changed.

"The vets I treated before didn't have to face improvised explosive devices, or people with bombs on their chests. It wasn't part of warfare then. The warfare of that era consisted of land mines, guns. Maybe they had grenades but nothing like this stuff these guys use now. That's changed the nature of the injuries we see today."

Dr. Pollack provides insight about how the Road Home Program has evolved and how treatment modalities have evolved as well.

"Originally, the only veterans working at Road Home were on the outreach team. We would make a solid connection, build trust, the veteran would come in for an appointment, and we never saw them again. As the Road Home Program evolved, we found it paramount that we have veteran representation throughout our treatment process.

"As we learned more about veterans, we realized the value of EBP and continue to provide treatment strategies based upon the latest advances in research training and, most important, group therapy. We realize the value of trust and build our environment around that trust. We create a safe zone, safe harbor, if you will, where veterans and their families can come to a nonthreatening, nonjudgmental environment. We call these early visits "touches." We talk about difficulties and challenges, but we also put a lot of effort into bringing out veterans' strengths. Despite the horrors they have experienced, there is a lot of goodness and positive aspects to military service."

And what are some of the evidence based practice latest techniques being used?

"We have been using exposure therapy and it has been very effective. Basically, instead of trying to push the horrific events into the past, exposure therapy allows us to have the veteran confront and relive the activity. By facing these challenges head on, we have learned that over time, the effects of PTSD begin to diminish. And by using virtual reality, this therapy helps the veteran overcome these memories. Building self-esteem and confidence, as well as more restful sleep, are the benefits we have realized."

I know of many veterans' success stories from the Road Home Program. None are better than this one from the Road Home Facebook page:

> I spent three weeks going through their Intense PTSD treatment program. I went with the hope that I would leave encouraged to get out of the house and be more active. What I left with was a greater understanding of my trauma and how it has been affecting my life in a negative way. I received so much more than I ever expected from this program. I came home with a new passion for life and a new drive for a new ministry. I have not had this drive or passion for many years. I am ready to start living life again and enjoying the things that God has given me. After returning home from this great program I finally decided to overcome my fear, stop living in the past and no longer live in a "It could have been" life. What I learned and accepted in treatment gave me the courage to start living life again.[8]

Marine Corporal Bea Kenny's experience gives credence to the knotty problem of diagnosis and treatment. Bea told me that the EN-Abled Vet internship "cured" her PTSD. I was highly skeptical. Granted, I am not a psychologist, but it seemed clear to me that a work therapy program, designed to teach IT skills, could hardly result in a cure.

My internship is designed to provide an opportunity to get a job, certainly not to be a therapy session. I told Dr. Karnik Bea's story, and to my surprise, he said that the internship probably *did cure her PTSD*. I was floored!

Dr. Karnik explained that her EN-Abled Vet internship *was therapy* for Bea and along with her participation in other programs, her PTSD could be cured, or at the very least, became a lot more manageable. It was at his point that I realized that a compendium of modalities and treatments were key to treatment, including family, evidenced base practice, and new strategies.

You be the judge. What about this veteran? Is her PTSD cured?

11

YOU CURED MY PTSD?

Being strong means taking one more step toward the top of the hill, no matter how weary you may be. It means letting the tears flow through the grief. It means to keep looking for the answer, though the darkness of despair is all around you.[1]

—Historian John M. Marshall III

OK, I will be the first to admit that the title of this chapter is pretty strong and misleading. And it would appear that there is significant evidence in the literature that PTSD cannot be cured.[2] Nothing can change or erase the traumatic event or events that triggered PTSD in the first place.

After speaking with several psychologists and psychologists, I understand that PTSD cannot be cured, but the symptoms and potential triggers can be effectively managed by medication, therapy, and support. What I didn't realize was that workplace support can also be a strategy in minimizing the effects of PTSD—not as a standalone and certainly not a cure—but a warm, receptive, and caring environment, found in most hospitals and other service types of organizations, can be an adjunct to each other.

Such is the story of Bea.

"My name is Bogumila Kenny and I am in the EN-Abled Veteran Internship. My friends call me "Bea." I am from Eastern Europe where I was a potato farmer. I went to a small school there where pitching in on a farm was more important than studying. But I always wanted to learn.

"I moved to Chicago with my family when I was thirteen, which was a great culture shock for me. I spoke no English, so I would study seven days a week and I worked very hard to learn the language. I had a great teacher that would help me with English and math written problems. I wanted to study hard and be everything American.

83

"I joined the Marine Corps for the love of this country. I couldn't believe it when the Marines took me in and accepted me, so I wanted to give something back. I was in the Marines for six years. I wanted to make a career out of service, but in 2012 I was medically boarded out of the service with an honorable discharge.

"Transitioning out of the Marines was very difficult as I was the only person in my unit who was deployed. Consequently, my command did not know how to deal with me. After a number of counselling and psychiatry appointments, I knew I couldn't do what they wanted me to do anymore.

"As I transitioned, the only advice I really got was 'Don't wear a loud suit to the interview. Wear green, it is the safest color and make sure you wear a bobbed haircut, because it makes you look more professional.' I did get some resume training, but I thought the resume wasn't good enough to get me a job. We did work together to change some military lingo so that others could understand, but that was about it.

"I did end up going to school but I had difficulties with my PTSD and anxiety. I was able to keep the schedule with an online university, and with my therapy dog at my side, I could complete the coursework. I was desperate to graduate. Because of my disability, I couldn't interact with others very well and often just stayed at home. I had to have a controlled environment so that I could focus on my work. I wanted to still be the same person I was in the Marine Corps.

"After I was discharged, I was diagnosed with Hashimoto's disease, which physically messed up my perceptions and thought processes. I learned it could lead to depression and lack of focus. So because I was diagnosed after discharge, I began to blame everything else in my life on Hashimoto's disease.

"I started to go into denial mode. You know, I am such a strong person. I grew up in the Eastern bloc under pretty stressful circumstances. You couldn't trust your government, you couldn't trust your neighbors, and well after the Berlin Wall fell, my family was still eating only potatoes and milk every day. I grew up a tough person, so I started to believe that no way could a strong person like me have something like PTSD. I believed everything happened to me to be purely chemical.

"I had my eye on getting a cybersecurity job, but in the meantime, I began working at Starbucks. At Starbucks, everyone there treated me very well—they even gave me an apron with a flag on it because I was a Marine. Their training was very similar to military training where you're told to do specific tasks in a specific way and they also had training manuals, just like military training.

"Starbucks did everything they possibly could for me, but because of the intense interaction with customers and coworkers, I failed. I'm the type of person where I try to hide any weakness. Until a couple of months ago, my family didn't know I was sick because it's embarrassing to me. They figured that I had dropped off the face of the earth for the time being. Only my husband knew.

"I was so stressed out that I started to experience physical pain as well as nightmares, full on flashbacks, tunnel vision, sharp chest pains, accelerated respiration. My face and arms went numb.

"I got offered a job working in cybersecurity for the FBI, but because of my current state, I was unable to complete the necessary paperwork before being hired. I could go no further. At that point, my husband drove me to the VA hospital. I walked in there crying and it was discovered that my blood pressure was dangerously high. Still, it was my husband who dragged me in there because I really didn't want to speak to anybody on my own.

"My husband of eleven years has been incredible and we have a very stable relationship. In fact, if I feel that I am not being honest with my doctor and that I may be hiding something, my new strategy is to bring my husband along and ask him to tell the doctor because I don't feel that I have been communicating with him and I think I am underselling what is going on. I did that because it made me feel more normal.

"It was then that I decided that I needed to get help. I began treatment for PTSD and anxiety with the intent that I was going to be a police officer. I had the mentality that I was going to recover from this. Sure, I knew that I need to be off my medications before I could return to military or federal service and the FBI, so I was determined to get off this medicine as quickly as I could.

"So I tapered off responsibly, but I put pressure on the doctors to try to convince them I was OK. It wasn't a lie because I was truly convinced that I was OK and I was able to convince everybody that I was OK. So I got off my practice pretty quickly.

"I did well with interviews, but every time I got close to being hired, my anxiety kicked back in and I was not doing well during the final one-on-one interviews So, I figured, well, I'll just get better with more practice. Thinking about it now I realize that it was my disability that was holding me back.

"I did get a job at the DOJ, and you know what? Everybody loved me as I am a hard worker. Two weeks into the job, my vision started to fail, I started to get dizzy, and I was vomiting every day before I went to work. One day on the job, I was put in a room with some very dangerous people that I was supposed to interact with. Now I was not a stranger to danger during my military career. My job was to deliver ammunitions and explosives to the front line. Not for a moment did I ever believe that I was going to come back to the United States alive. It didn't really matter what happened to me. If I were to die, it was my job to save as many Marines as possible. But things were different with the DOJ. I suddenly started to think about what would happen if I got hurt on the job. I feared for my safety and my travel to downtown Chicago every day. I expressed my feelings to my bosses that I couldn't be part of a team and make it weaker. Looking back, I'm glad I got to go through that experience because I fell flat on my face and realized, you know what, things change. Dust yourself off and go through the recovery process.

"So I pushed aside everything related to DEA, DOJ, FBI, and the police. On paper, I looked really good so I was getting a lot of interest. But if I'm going to keep getting these thoughts, I knew I couldn't repeat the same cycle of suppressing my PTSD and end up in the same place I am now.

"I turned my attention to software engineering and IT. I needed to do something to support my family so I went up to James A. Lovell Federal Healthcare Center again for help, throwing up along the way while taking the train. When I got to the Veterans Rehabilitation Unit at Lovell, I was standing in the doorway debating whether or not I would hide things or come clean and tell people I was really sick.

"When I walked in there I said, 'You know what? I'm going to tell you the truth. I just threw up out of nervousness. This is what happens to me because I'm really really sick and I'm very anxious about meeting new people. I'm forcing myself to do this because I want to recover and be really successful. But I want you to know that this is happening.'

"And gosh! The VA staff really relaxed me. This is a professional who knows how to calm down an anxiety-filled Marine, that's for sure. So after the meeting, the honesty felt good, but it still felt foreign. They looked at my resume and we talked. The counselor said, 'I know this wonderful program called the EN-Abled Veteran Internship and we are going there for an interview and I will drive you there.

"My first reaction was what? OK, I know that place, super intimidating, because it is such a big prestigious name. Talk about scaring a girl. And go tomorrow? How am I going to prepare to meet new people? So I thought, 'Since I have been doing it this one way where I have not been honest with people and I don't talk about it, and only my husband knows me, I'm going to have to change my strategy full on and just do the exact opposite of my instincts and my character.'

"When I came to the EN-Abled Veteran Internship, I had one of two directions to take. I could either omit and put on the show that everybody loves because people do love me. I'm professional, focused, and on paper I'm awesome. My other option was just to be honest. So I showed up. I figured it would be intimidating, but my doctor said, 'just take your anxiety practice, try to relax, don't rush, wake up a little earlier, and take your morning stroll.' My expectations when I got here was that there's no way they are going to hire me. I didn't have much job experience, and I was thinking so negative. But when Jaime said to me, 'We value aptitude,' that totally relaxed me, because I knew I had the aptitude.

"My first few days I was expecting to get overwhelmed and end up in mental health, with all my symptoms at maximum ten and not making it through this program all the way. That was my mentality. It started to change, when I understood people's reaction to me.

"The first one to reach out to me was Marlene and she was a civilian. I didn't really want to talk too much for fear of saying something wrong. I didn't know if she would like me. But she was so awesome to me. One day, she invited me to lunch. Now that's her private time when she gets to relax, yet she invites me there and then I meet her coworkers that like to lunch together. When I said to them, 'I'm in the EN-Abled Veteran Internship; I am a Marine veteran,' I expected something else but they were like, 'wow that's really cool, huh!'

"They didn't stick to asking me about military stuff, which was what I expected. Kiesha was there and I found her to be one of the most inviting, bubbly, friendly personalities you could imagine. Usually, once I tell people I am a female Marine, which is extraordinary, it kind of stops there. People don't like to ask me anything about anything else but being a Marine. So when you say you're a Marine that's your identity now and forever.

"Instead they started asking me things like, 'Did you try that cookie. What's your favorite food? Where's your accent from? What do you mean there are more than two types of potatoes?' All of a sudden, they are treating me like I'm more than just a female Marine. They opened up to me and they kept including me and inviting me to lunch. They told me jokes. I wasn't the center of attention and I wasn't off to the side, I was just sort of in the mix and I felt normal, which is such a weird thing to say.

"I definitely felt valued because they were talking about how I have what it takes to make it in IT and that this is the place to get a lot of things on my resume. It was nice because I don't make friends easily and this was more like girlfriends talking. It's been *so* long since I was in society. Previously, my social life was to cook when my husband's friends came over and stay in the background while they played video games. Now, all of a sudden, I wanted to talk and I wanted to interact with the group. It was really cool!

"There were weekly veterans' meetings in the Information Services Department, chaired by Jaime, that were such an important thing for me because they helped me gauge my environment. So I'm sitting there and one of the other veterans is telling his story, saying that with his disability, the work environment was hurting him. But he also said, 'It is being addressed and fixed and I am improving now.' Then another veteran stated, 'I'm not going to talk about my disability. I'm just here to get the training and get the job.' Neither one of these approaches are wrong, it's just up to the individual.

"And at that point, I just let everything go. I am so introverted, so reserved, don't make friends or like being around people because it gives me anxiety. But the weekly EN-Abled Veteran meetings was such an open environment for me that I felt like I could overcome things there. The opportunity to approach leadership in a welcoming environment was incredible.

"I learned from the EN-Abled Veteran Internship was that I can do this. Karim was my team leader who just didn't go 'click yes' or 'click no' this or that. He took the time and went into the background, *mind you he is very busy as can be*. But I got hands-on experience and remembered that you [Jaime] said I already had the aptitude.

"I learned how to image computers. I was able to install the proper software, set up passwords, deal with joining the equipment to the domain, which is very different for every computer and every client. I actively participated in a deployment, which was pretty cool to interact with the customers outside of IT. But the coolest thing, I thought, was when I plugged in a personal computer and beeps start going off. Karim explained to me what was wrong and how to fix it. I learned how to pull a machine apart, put different parts back in, run system checks, etc. Soon I began messing around with hardware, which was really cool. I got so much experience that I added an entire page to my resume. And it's really cool to be replacing my military stuff on my resume with what I had learned on the job. I had listed all of my medals and awards [*laughs*]. Now that I think about it, wow, what was I doing?

"I started to believe that I was making a really good civilian because I was working well on a civilian team. I was the only military person when I went out to hook up a couple of computers and problem solve help desk tickets and help with other customer needs. It was really a cool experience to walk around interact with the nurses and realize that you are doing something right now that is really improving patients' lives. That's a calling and that's really cool. You're not like, oh, I'm working and I am making some rich guy richer. No, you fix the printer for the prescriptions and all of a sudden that patient gets to go home a little earlier. It's great to fix a computer for a doctor so that he or she doesn't have to worry or try to fix it themselves. It was really cool to be a small piece of the puzzle that makes people healthier.

"This is a huge awesome community. Everyone focuses on making people feel welcome and veterans become the best versions of themselves. I don't think it's just the program, it's also the community. It was really awesome the way that the staff was trained before I was coming. I never got a look like, 'Oh, you're a Marine? Did you ever kill anybody?' Or you get that look where people see you are a disabled Marine and immediately think, oh, is this going to be some kind of problem? None of that fear exists in the EN-Abled Veteran Internship.

"Like most people with PTSD, I don't have a temper. I internalize most of the time because I don't want to make people around me uncomfortable. Sometimes people actually say that I need to be more assertive. I found a happy balance with the EN-Abled Veteran Internship, where now I learned how to interact with people and I feel like I'm a civilian, which is a good feeling!

"As the days passed, I felt more comfortable, so comfortable that I started taking less practice. There is some satisfaction in feeling like you're working again in a safe place, which, essentially for me, was home. Feeling that you aren't contributing to society is the most difficult part of military transition. When you leave military service, you feel like you fall off the face of the earth and that you are no longer contributing to society. Here at the EN-Abled Veteran Internship, I am making the world a better place by making sick people better again. No, I'm not a doctor, but I'm part of a team that supports the doctor. I feel that support is just as important. Sometimes I was feeling so good at work, I wouldn't want to leave my safe haven and go home at night. This was work therapy for me and I wouldn't want to get on the train and it's a personal hell to get back home. This is crazy!

"When I first started and got on the train, I would sweat and my heart would pound, and I would have sharp chest pains, get sick to my stomach, and throw up. I call it my PTSD throw ups. Not a lot of people find that funny. On the train, I couldn't concentrate. I had tunnel vision, I felt like the danger was right around the corner at every moment. I was honest about this at the EN-Abled Veteran Internship, which made me be more honest with my doctor.

"I don't know when it happened, but a few weeks ago I missed my stop because I forgot I was sitting on a train. Being on my phone and forgetting I was on the train was an incredible breakthrough. I was no longer anxious on the train! What helped me was I was honest about it here because it's therapeutic here. My doctor told me 'Do the math. You're a very logic-driven person. Do the math. You're afraid of a mass attack on a transit system, or somebody pushing you off the blue line so you land on the electric rail below. Why don't you just do the math?'

"I think that was happening with the news and media, we eat doom and gloom. We eat it up and they keep serving it to us. But statistically speaking, I realized that I have a much better chance of winning the lottery than something bad happening to me on the way to work. I became desensitized to the train ride. I would have not been able to accomplish this long term if the atmosphere of the EN-Abled Veteran Internship was not correct. I would have failed. The repetition over time and being able to communicate with Karim helped me. Sometimes, Karim would just look at me and say 'tough ride?' I would say, 'Yeah.' He would say, 'why don't you sit down for a while with a cool beverage.' Once he knew I was a little better, he would give me a task with some computers. And I would feel better.

"If you would tell me I would ever feel comfortable on the train, I would *never* have believed you. I sat in front of the doctors since 2008 mind you, talking about PTSD and talking about it and talking about it and it meant nothing to me. I know these people at the VA try but what helped me achieve successful recovery was doing hands-on work in the EN-Abled Veteran Internship. Through all those years at the VA I had no significant recovery. I didn't have to face any of my weaknesses at work because I would quit or work around it. My VA therapy wasn't productive because I didn't know that I had a lot of issues, because like everybody, you try to avoid pain. You steer away from it to the point where one day you end up locking yourself in your house and become agoraphobic. And I was very close to that, I gotta tell you, I was very close to that.

"But here I realized I was doing a good job and I was able to concentrate. People were valuing my work and I felt like I was contributing to a team. I realized that I was actually doing a big chunk of the daily work. I'm not in on Fridays and on Mondays, Karim says, 'Man, it's a lot easier on me when you are here. I was so stressed out because of the extra work. You are doing something that helps me so much.' So all of a sudden, I'm thinking, man, I'm making a difference and I'm actually getting the confidence that I need to do well in interviews. It's not just talking about, oh, you're a valuable person, you are very smart, and one day you are going to be very successful and I'm sure you're going to recover. I was actually doing it!

"For someone like me I was completely out of touch. I didn't know how to fit back in; I didn't know how to go about it, but when I was sitting in front of doctors [who were] talking about how awesome and valuable a person I was, I didn't believe any of it. I didn't have a single positive inner dialogue thought within myself about, you know, you're going to be in IT and you're going to be successful. The only thing is I thought was, well, I went to this online college, like every Marine and now my resume is just like every other Marine, and I'm probably going to end up working at Starbucks. No, wait, I can't because it physically hurts me and so what am I gonna do?

"I had tried everything on my own, believe me. I applied to over seventy places on USAjobs.gov. I created a spreadsheet of where I was applying in the civilian world. I wasn't doing it right. Looking for a job became a new anxiety that put me back on practice because looking for a job was such a high stressful thing for me. Filling out applications stressed me out so much that sometimes my husband would say, 'enough for today.' I didn't know how to go about it. I was lost. I didn't know what to do because I had no guidance.

"I got the computer degree but I did not think I was going to work in IT. Seriously. Before I found meaningful work, I had no other identity, just a Marine, going to the VA to talk about it. It was not working and it didn't bring me out of my complete disconnection because of my limitations. It didn't help me feel normal.

"Here, I feel normal. This program helped me heal. If the VA could understand that I did more healing with this program in two and a half months than I did in their system for years and years and years, that would be the motivation to get the unemployment rate down. Going to the VA to talk about it does not make me feel normal. It made me feel definitely separate from society. It did not make me feel more confident; it made me feel more broken.

"The VA staff are really good people; they tried to help me and I understand. But the approach for someone like me must be put me to work. Please, just put me to work. If I didn't find meaningful work, my alternative was to go all the way to the VA and work at the VA doing janitorial stuff to get back in the swing of things on how to work and how to interact with people. That would not have made me feel more normal, that would have made me feel like a bunch of broken veterans, including myself, at the

VA hospital doing janitorial duties in order to one day be able to work. And that would have not worked for me because I am too ambitious."

Bea's story brings to light a lot of anguish, frustration, and success. While the VA has been the subject of negative press, and perhaps, privatization, what is the current state of the VA and what is happening to support this new generation of veterans?

12

NOT YOUR FATHER'S VA

He's such a flirt. He needs ten hugs before he gets out of there.[1]

—Valerie Shaffer, wife of sixty-year-old
Viet Nam veteran Joseph Shaffer

The Veterans Administration is proud of its long and storied history of supporting our nation's military, spanning almost four hundred years. According to the Department of Veterans Affairs website:

> The United States has the most comprehensive system of assistance for Veterans of any nation in the world, with roots that can be traced back to 1636, when the Pilgrims of Plymouth Colony were at war with the Pequot Indians. The Pilgrims passed a law that stated that disabled soldiers would be supported by the colony. Later, the Continental Congress of 1776 encouraged enlistments during the Revolutionary War, providing pensions to disabled soldiers. In the early days of the Republic, individual states and communities provided direct medical and hospital care to Veterans. In 1811, the federal government authorized the first domiciliary and medical facility for Veterans. Also, in the 19th century, the nation's Veterans assistance program was expanded to include benefits and pensions not only for Veterans, but for their widows and dependents.[2]

A quick look shows that "about $72 billion of VA's budget this fiscal year [2018] goes to medical care, and the department has more than 1,200 medical facilities nationwide."[3] "The VA health care system has grown from 54 hospitals in 1930 to 1,600 health care facilities today, including 144 VA Medical Centers and 1,232 outpatient care centers."[4]

But how is the VA doing in supporting military veterans today? In 2016 the Pew Research Center conducted a survey to assess the public's view of the state of U.S. politics and various government agencies. While the public continues to express favorable views of many federal agencies and departments, "the Department of Veterans Affairs (VA) receives the lowest favorability rating for the departments and agencies in the survey—49% view it favorably while 34% have an unfavorable opinion."[5] A lot of noise has been generated both pro and con in evaluating how effective the VA is in helping its patients and customers, and some of this has spilled over to the political arena where some efforts have been made to privatized healthcare services.

And no wonder. In a recent five-day period, the VA's Office of Inspector General released a series of reports detailing the state of VA healthcare (see figure 12.1).

To get a personal read on all of this and how the VA has changed, I turned back to my VA partner, Dee Barnes, who received VA benefits for the last twenty-one years as well as dedicated her post-military life to helping veterans get the benefits they need and have earned.

"There are two components of VRU, the education component and the employment side. Veterans can apply for educational assistance through

Recently Released Reports[i]

	Recently Released Reports
09/17/2018	Comprehensive Healthcare Inspection Program Review of the Roseburg VA Health Care System, Oregon
09/13/2018	Delays and Deficiencies in Obtaining and Documenting Mammography Services at the Atlanta VA Health Care System, Decatur, Georgia
09/12/2018	Inpatient Security, Safety, and Patient Care Concerns at the Chillicothe VA Medical Center, Ohio
09/12/2018	Illicit Fentanyl Use and Urine Drug Screening Practices in a Domiciliary Residential Rehabilitation Treatment Program at the Bath VA Medical Center, New York
09/12/2018	Leasing Procedures Used to Acquire VA's Wilmington Health Care Center
09/12/2018	Comprehensive Healthcare Inspection Program Review of the Battle Creek VA Medical Center, Michigan

[i] https://www.va.gov/oig/, retrieved September 17, 2018

Figure 12.1.   Reports Released by the VA Office of Inspector General during September 2018.

the VRU, which conducts an educational assessment to determine if their disabilities hinder their ability to perform similar jobs in the civilian sector. Based upon the assessment and their desires, veterans can receive additional educational or vocational benefits that enable them to find gainful employment matching their capabilities and potential.

"Upon completion of such training, the other side of the VRU assists with helping them find jobs in their local communities. When you join the service, military personnel never have to market themselves. Based upon job performance, time of service, and individual study, military members move up pay and grade with increasing leadership scope and opportunities. Resumes, job interviews, and other soft skills are simply not in place and therefore are never learned or applied. Upon leaving military service, this lack of experience in the job search hurts veterans' chances for civilian employment. By the time they leave the military, non-veterans have a distinct advantage over the military veteran who has never had to compete for a job. Consequently, many veterans lack basic hard and soft skills in the job chasing game that become differentiators in job selection. Having never participated in a competitive job market before, veterans lack basic skills in resume building, social media searching, job interview skills, social cues, and other important cultural aspects of competing for and winning a job. The VRU has skilled professionals who take a one-on-one approach in walking veterans through all aspects of the job searching culture. Other types of assistance include selecting appropriate clothing and paying for, as an example, work boots if an individual gets a construction job.

"In addition, veterans may have deep-seated issues or disabilities that hinder their chances for employment. Some veterans may have PTSD, substance abuse problems, transitioning difficulties, money worries, or divorce and broken family circumstances. The VRU takes on these veterans and helps them through personal and family struggles in order to help them get back on their feet and into the workforce.

"In lieu of a hiring organization recruiting and paying a veteran's wages, the VRU enters into an agreement with the hiring organization where that organization will pay the veteran's wage through the VRU. For example, during the EN-Abled Veteran internship, we would pay the VRU a $12.50/hr. stipend, thirty-two hours a week for twelve weeks for each veteran in our program. The VRU would pay the veteran $11.50/hr., keeping $1/hr. to help pay for various administrative components of the VRU program (such as funding for work boots as previously mentioned). By using this mechanism, veterans could also take advantage of other benefits. For example, veterans in the VRU program could receive a dental benefit, something that they would not receive as a part-time employee at Rush. Healthcare payments were also not a concern because the veteran could use their medical benefit regardless of their VRU status. This also helps them to avoid paying for healthcare at Rush, which they aren't eligible for given their part-time status. All in all, it makes for a clean way for veterans to get paid, the VRU program to function, and to provide the maximum benefit for the military veteran."

Dee's program is very effective, yet you may be wondering where the military is when it comes to providing transitioning services and why so much is left to the VA? During my research, I found that there are programs in place for military personnel during their service discharge process, but these programs are not all-inclusive and lack standardization and consistency across all branches. While the military does an outstanding job at onboarding and training its military, the four services (reporting through the Department of Defense) and the Coast Guard (who reports to the Department of Transportation) drop the ball when they release service members. The military trains the service member how to climb aboard and fight, but not how to get off and leave. It is disappointing to note that there is no real congruency between the four branches of service and the VA, a situation that historically reflects the difference between two branches of government with distinct funding streams as directed by Congress.

There are five transition assistance programs that funnel into a single VA system of support.

- Army, The Soldier for Life—Transition Assistance Program
  https://www.sfl-tap.army.mil
- Air Force, Transition Assistance Program
  https://www.afpc.af.mil/Separation/Transition-Assistance-Program/
- Navy, Transition GPS
  https://www.public.navy.mil/bupers-npc/career/transition/Pages/TAP.aspx
- Marine for Life Cycle
  http://www.usmc-mccs.org/services/career/transition-readiness/
- Coast Guard, Office of Work-Life, Transition Assistance Program
  https://www.dcms.uscg.mil/Our-Organization/Assistant
  -Commandant-for-Human-Resources-CG-1/Health-Safety
  -and-Work-Life-CG-11/Office-of-Work-Life-CG-111/
  Transition-Assistance-Program/

Since 9/11, the VA has shifted focus and put resources and programs toward many of the most compelling and direct needs of the veterans coming back from Afghanistan and the Middle East. The VA has put tremendous efforts into addressing the problem of homeless veterans, something that was lacking following previous wars. Sexual trauma support programs and PTSD and TBI assessment and treatment programs have been established and well-resourced in all fifty states. Veterans can come in and attend eight- to twelve-week programs to help them cope with things that have happened to them in the military. The results have been positive and supportive for these veterans who may have been forgotten or misunderstood decades ago.

III

THE TWENTY-FIRST-CENTURY VETERAN

13

MINORITY REPORT

I am uncomfortable in a group now because I'm easily bored with discussions of babies, food prices and home-making problems. People seem to be living behind walls, with no interest in national or international events . . . and they look at you strangely if you discuss any current problem other than what they are going to have for breakfast the next morning.[1]

—Female veteran surveyed for a master's
thesis on readjustment, 1947

Often neglected and universally unappreciated, women have been key components in the military going all the way back to the American Revolution. "In recent years, the number of women in the military has steadily increased to more than 200,000, which is about 14.5 percent of those in active duty, according to the Pentagon. However, women have always been part of the war effort, whether directly or indirectly. When men went overseas to war, women often stepped in to fill their vacancies during World War I and II. Women have also been recognized for their medical services to wounded soldiers since Clara Barton nursed soldiers during the Civil War."[2]

The National Veterans Foundation lists four major hurdles female veterans face when they leave service:

1. Damaging stereotypes
2. A VA that's geared toward male veterans
3. A civilian population that doesn't get female soldiers
4. Transition programs that are also geared toward men

In the conclusion of a report highlighting aspects of the transition home that are unique to women, the author observes, "We can only hope the VA updates its programs and services. The public also needs to adjust its vision of what and who soldiers and veterans really are. The military can also play an important role in helping with the female veteran's transition to civilian life."[3]

Throughout history, American servicewomen have fought in battlefields, serving and dying for their country. Female gladiators, Viking shield maidens, and even Native American women who fought Christopher Columbus have been documented in history.[4]

> While the oldest military service does not officially state who the first [U.S.] woman to join its ranks was, most historians agree that it was Deborah Sampson. An indentured servant, Sampson joined the Continental Army in May 1781—though some reports place the year at 1782—and because women were not permitted to serve in the military, she disguised herself as a man by the name of Robert Shurtleff. Sampson was injured multiple times, sustaining a sabre wound to her head and a gunshot wound to her thigh that she treated herself for fear that her secret would be discovered if she sought medical attention.[5]

During World War II, "approximately 400,000 U.S. women served with the armed forces and more than 460—some sources say the figure is closer to 543—lost their lives as a result of the war, including 16 from enemy fire."[6] The core combination of ability and self-confidence allowed women veterans to successfully challenge and conquer social and economic convention.

"According to contemporary scholarship by D'Ann Campbell, 45 percent of nurses and 27 percent of women in other military fields" chose not to marry compared to 5 percent of nonmilitary women who chose the marriageless option. "This was a striking rejection of contemporary norms and a preface for a future in which professional careers would increasingly compete for the time of American women. It was also remarkable to the extent that it was a personal decision to invoke both social and economic change." Without a whimper from Washington, women, on their own, made these astonishing changes all by themselves, paving the way for the generations of women to come to seek equality in all aspects of life.[7]

As of 2015, "women comprised 15.3% of our active-duty military; 73% of them have served in combat or been exposed to dead, dying or wounded, so PTSD is common. Forty percent of military women have experienced MST (Military Sexual Trauma) while 67% have experienced sexual harassment. And these figures don't include unreported cases. Multiple studies show that PTSD from MST is twice as severe as combat PTSD. Women who have experienced MST as well as combat are particularly affected."[8]

We have only hurt ourselves and our country by proclaiming men should decide if, when, and where American servicewomen should be serving their country. Some of us believe that women have no business being in a warzone, even if they are far away from the front lines. Over the last three hundred plus years, we have created and evolved the reasons why women should not get equal opportunity and politicized a topic where the mettle of women in dangerous situations has been proven over and over again. Men look the other way when barriers of culture, politics, and bias have already been broken. We only hurt ourselves by denying women equal rights in areas where competency has already been proven.

In 2014, a *Washington Post*–Kaiser poll "interviewed a random national sample of 819 adults who served in Iraq or Afghanistan since Sept. 11, 2001, including 661 men and 158 women. The results from the survey have a margin of sampling error of plus or minus five percentage points overall, five points for men and 11 points for women."[9] Several key findings of the study are listed below:

- Female veterans from Iraq and Afghanistan have returned from war facing heightened family and emotional strains compared with their male counterparts.
- Nearly a quarter of women who served in Iraq or Afghanistan reported a sexual assault, according to a study from the Department of Veterans Affairs.
- Female veterans have mixed views of whether the military is or is not doing enough to prevent sexual assault, by 50 to 48 percent.
- Men on the other hand, are more apt to say enough is being done by a 55 to 40 percent margin.
- Women are suffering more than men when it comes to family problems and emotional health. Fifty-six percent of female service members say they have often or sometimes experienced relationship problems with their spouse as a result of their military service, compared with 44 percent of men.
- Women are more than twice as likely as men to say they are having problems with their children (39 percent for women to 16 percent for men) because of their service.
- War wounds extend beyond the physical for women as well. More than four in ten women returned from Iraq and Afghanistan

reporting worse mental and emotional health, compared with three in ten men.

- More than eight in ten women served in combat support roles, well above the 53 percent of men in that capacity.
- That gap is larger for men and women in combat support roles; 46 percent of women claim worse mental health compared with 25 percent for men in combat support.[10]

Tanjilisa Williams, who is African American, tells of her five and a half years in the Air Force, virtually all of it overseas.

"I dropped out of the University of Arkansas and joined right after 9/11 because I had a strong need and urge to do something and protecting my country and performing military service. I worked in ammunitions in my career, and I got out six months early because I was going to have a baby. As an ammo troop, we were in charge of testing, storing, and transporting ammunitions for the bases. Our operations were always several miles away from base, which I believe made us much closer together.

"I enjoyed my time in the military. After tech school, I spent two years in Fairford, England, and later moved to an airbase in Japan. I was young, twenty-two, had never been overseas before, and I really enjoyed the friends and comradery I was a part of during my abbreviated military career. I think every American should live outside the country and gain the experience of Americans not being the center of the universe.

"The military culture just really took hold of me and it was amazing how close-knit everyone was. We just got along, different races, backgrounds, religions, it just didn't matter. We were a family. I remember coming back to the states and I was just so surprised; I mean I was literally shocked when I heard the news and heard some friends still talking about racism. It was just a shock because overseas in the military, we didn't really experience that. The British didn't view us as blacks, they thought us all as Yankees and they didn't bother to subcategorize who we were. So it was just a really nice experience."

Marine Bea Kenney, who is white, had a similar experience. "During my career, I was never singled out for being anything but a Marine. I felt completely safe my entire career. Often times, I was the only woman in a large group of men. No man ever said anything or did anything inappropriate. We were all just Marines and we had everybody's back."

However, Army Sergeant Cassandra Taylor had a completely different experience. "I joined the military in November, 17, 1985, and served twenty-eight years in the Army Reserves. I joined the Army because I was running away from a guy I had been dating. He had a hold on my mind . . . nothing physical, nothing abusive. But I had a four-year-old girl at the time and I felt that I just had to make a change and get away. Because I had a daughter and didn't want to give up custody to my parents, I went reserve instead of active duty.

"I joined the Army to get educated and get paid at the same time. I enjoyed 95 percent of my twenty-eight years in the Reserves and I'd do it all over again. One thing about me is I often spoke out a lot in the military for what I thought was right and what I thought needed to be said. It's who I was then, and who I am now. I've learned to do it better over the years—the best way to tell someone that they were wrong.

"About twelve years ago, I was at a club and a drunk soldier grabbed my breasts from behind, saying, 'I've been waiting to do this ever since I met you,' Now I did not hit him. You see, I always have my kids, my career, and my job to think about. I didn't want to lose my job and I didn't want to go to jail.

"My reaction was a hurt look and disbelief. His first sergeant stepped in immediately and apologized on the spot. 'Don't mess up his career,' he said. 'He's just drunk.' Next day, the guy came around and he, too, apologized. 'I'm sorry I was drunk.' But for me it wasn't a matter of 'I'm sorry I was drunk.'

"The crazy part to all of this was there were a lot of other black male soldiers there. And they jokingly said, 'Well, you know, Cassandra, he just said something that we've been wanting to do ever since *we* met you and *we* say it when we're sober, ha, ha, ha.'

"And I said, '*It's not funny.*' And they played it off, like, oh, we were just trying to make light of the situation. Do you want us to hurt him? And I said no.

"What's that saying, 'a drunk man speaks a sober mind?' I don't believe he meant to do any harm. I believe he actually wanted to squeeze and he didn't think about whether it was harmful or not. I believe his thought was, I just want to squeeze them. Period. No aftermath. No thought process about how it makes a woman feel and that's the difference between being a boy in the military and a woman in the military. I know I'm stereotyping and I really shouldn't do that. But it's true 95 percent of the time. But I still go to therapy for my MST today.

"What women have to deal with in the Army is not just sexism from men, but sexism from other women. I'm treated differently whenever I'm approached by another woman. It's like the jealousy stuff comes in and you try not to get into that because that's the first thing that comes out of a woman's mouth when she is having a conflict with other women. But I was ahead of other people. I had my master's degree. I was likable, and I was friendly and I had connections with people in higher places and that was a point of contention with my female boss.

"My boss tried to ruin my career. In 2012, she revictimized me—more of a mental MST. She was trying to rape my mind. It was victimization. It's a sexual PTSD. Plus, I had other medical issues, high blood pressure, anxiety, fear of losing my job. But you know what? I survived her. I have accomplished more and received more from what she did to me if we hadn't worked together in the first place. It's funny how that happens.

"An investigation ensued and the EOE [Equal Opportunity Employer] officer agreed with all of this. I could have done a few more years, but I got out. Then, I found out that the post office didn't keep my job. I was gone too long, and after five years they give away your position. I can understand that as I had been gone twelve years and they can't hold my position open that long. But what surprised me was, I thought I could go back be a post office employee, but no.

"If a woman is on the job they need to work hard. Boys are distracted by an attractive woman, and all work stops when one walks by. For women, it's different. We may see a handsome man walk by but we're interested in other things, things that you can't see. We've got to talk and get to know the man. On the other hand, men are just ready to go.

"I have a T-shirt I like to wear that says 'Serve Like a Girl.' There is a big stigma being a girl in the military. We are breaking the glass cylinder but the stigma is still powerful. She can't do this. She's a lightweight. She gets emotional. She's a girl, she can't lift this. It's her time of the month.

"Now some of those things aren't true. Yes, 95 percent of girls don't have the physical strength of a man. But when it comes to technical mental stuff, oh yeah. Not that we can outthink you, but we can rationalize. We can think things through and accomplish things just like a man, if not better, when it comes down to things like that. I would never ever ever say physically a woman can outdo a man. But the stigma of not being offered a job, because she is a woman, to me is the worst thing any organization or any man can ever say.

"Because you'd be surprised. When put into a position, where a woman has to decide, we can do that because we know *how* to do that because we don't get emotional at that time. We know how to separate the two.

"It's harder for that woman to be that leader. She gotta work harder. She has to prove who we are. But a man came come in and just skate. He can come in, sign a few things, and goof off. But a woman has to prove it all the time and justify why [she is] good enough to do the job.

"Is there a stigma to being an African American in the Army? Yeah. We're lazy. We lazy. If there is anything you don't want us to know, put it in a book because y'all know that we don't know like to read. [We took a break here because we were both laughing so hard at Cassandra's obvious yet insightful joke.]

"Being black in America, I try to tell this to the young black men I run across. They always say 'the man got his foot on my neck, I'd never get the same treatment if I were a white guy,' well, why would you do anything if you already know that. 'You know that if you're black and you have two kilos on your possession, no license, a taillight out, and you got a gun, you know you're going to jail. If you're a white guy, the same thing, everything the same. He gets out, cuss[es] the police officer, you know he gets a slap on the wrist. He going home or getting two years in jail. You're not going to be treated the same; that's something we cannot change and accepting that we cannot change that that's the Serenity Prayer, but do better.

"Do what they don't expect you to do and that's to get educated. It's a fight. But we have to do that and it rolls into being a woman in the military. They don't expect us to pass. When I left Ft. McCoy, I completed my bachelor's, then I completed my master's. I completed all my military education in four years. After I exhausted that, I worked on civilian education.

"You were flipping burgers when you got it. What do you do now? What did you do in the military? Did you try to get any education? Did you get to bring anything home with you? No, I didn't. Well, shame on you. Don't get out until you got something tangible to show to the civilian world. Get all you can from the military. Period. Because they're going to get it from you. That was my mindset the entire twenty-eight years I was in. Get all you can. My body paid a toll, but I got all I could from Uncle Sam. And now that I'm out, he has paid everything back that I gave to him. And to me, it doesn't make sense to come into that Army and come out with nothing. Pimp Uncle Sam. Get your money. When it's time to send you to the sandbox, you've got this done. When you come home, you're ready for reality."

Dee Barnes is an employment specialist working in the VRU at the James A. Lovell Federal Health Care Center in North Chicago, Illinois. She was a logistic specialist with the Army. "As an African American female in the military, I heard stories of people of my ethnicity having bad stories in the military. I'm not gonna say it doesn't happen, but when I came into the military I had a clearance and because of that clearance it afforded me special jobs. I got really good assignments that people only dream of: Egypt,

Somalia, Haiti, and special assignments at Ft. Detrick as a special assistant to a lieutenant colonel. For me, the military was what I made it. I carried myself in a professional manner and was treated as such."

Mark Truitt knows what it's like to carry himself in a professional manner. Many of the veterans in the EN-Abled Veteran Internship have come to find themselves again. One such veteran is Mark Truitt. "I spent four years in the Army working in various missiles programs before leaving the service in 1984. I bounced around a couple of jobs after leaving military service. I always had a strong interest in computers but was never able to make much use of this skill. Eventually, I went to the VRU at the James A. Lovell Federal Health Care Center, in North Chicago. The VRU has a great working relationship with the EN-Abled Veteran Internship and the people at the VRU thought I would be a good fit.

"I did well on the interviews, talked about what the program was all about, and I saw a need to image computers and get into virtual desktops.* So at EN-Abled Veteran, I found my home. This was a job that I really wanted to do and the program was on a large scale that I knew this was for me. Plus, I was needed, which was very important to me. I got the opportunity to deploy these devices as well as hook them up to the network, and verify the network speed with specific software we were using. The whole thing about the EN-Abled Veteran Internship, it allowed me as a veteran who had an aptitude in IT to learn so much about the IT field at an operational level. It enhanced, solidified, and expanded my knowledge in ways I never imagined. We would have a meeting with Jaime Parent and the department heads every Thursday where we checkpoint where we're at, how we were doing, and were given a gentle reminder that very soon we needed to get a j-o-b.

"Yes, get a job and keep a job.

"I can't say enough about what this did for my life as a whole. After I left the internship within a month or so, a staffing firm called Palace Gate found me a job with a security firm. At Trustwave, I was a project coordinator where we would install network firewalls for a variety of clients, sometimes with as much as nine hundred machines to be installed. The people at Trustwave liked my work; they liked my dedication, but unfortunately, the contract ended after nine months. But Trustwave liked me so they kept me on doing other types of software projects and basic computer installation and repair.

---

* Virtual desktops are devices that replace traditional personal computers. Information is pushed from the data center to a lighter hardware platform which offers better performance.

"All during this time, Jaime kept in contact with me to see how I was doing and if I needed anything. This was really touching for me because Jaime is a very busy man. He didn't have to do this. But he said that I was now part of the EN-Abled Veteran 'alumni' program, where from time to time we'd reach out to each other.

"I can't tell you how important this was to me. The fact that a man of his stature and responsibilities would take time out of his busy day just to see how I was doing. He could have easily just figured, well, you're on your way, and that's the end of it. But no. This man was not going to let me go and he does the same thing with every veteran that comes through the internship. He would do everything he could do to keep me employed; he made it his business to ensure that whatever we needed from him, he would provide. And he put my resume on his expansive website that hit all of Chicagoland. He would also do stuff like use his LinkedIn pager to reach out to his eight thousand followers or keep putting our updated resume on his EN-Abled Veteran website. Whatever we needed to be successful, Jaime would find it for us.

"I now work at Brightstar where I keep all end user devices up and running—the whole nine yards. Because of my love of IT and my dedication to work, which was the direct result of the skills and culture from the EN-Abled Veteran Internship.

"My whole life has changed because this man took the time to reach out and help a down and out veteran. I was struggling and life was not looking too good for me. To be honest, I don't know where I would be without this internship. It saved my self-esteem. I'm grateful that Jaime reached out and wanted to truly help veterans. I don't know anybody else who would think about the veterans so much, take the time to build an internship, take whatever skills they had, and get them jobs. Jaime was finding jobs for veterans that didn't have any IT skills!

"What's interesting is my family started to notice changes in me. They saw a new spirit and sense of purpose in my life. My brother asked me one day, 'Mark, what's happened to you? You don't even sound like my brother no more. I can see that you, uh, what's the word I want to say? Yeah, you look like a professional. You found your niche.'

"I told them, 'Well, that's thanks to my white father.'

"'White father?? What are you talking about?'

"'Well, Jaime Parent has become my white father. And his wife, Tracy, is in there too—she's my white mother. They took me under their wing and, well, I told my white father that his black son is working hard and doing great. We hug, laugh, and cry at the same time.

"I can't express enough gratitude. Who gets an opportunity to do something they love doing and getting paid for it at the same time. I go to work happy every day because I'm doing the things I always wanted to do. IT is always changing; you always learn something new.

"A healthy and accepting place of work is bringing me and my family back together. It has made me a better man."

The last word is left for the Institute for Veterans and Military Families:

Sociologists now often say that the U.S. military is a model of good race relations. Although there is no denying progress made in military race relations, especially since establishment of the all-volunteer force, this review challenges that comfortable claim as research done over the past two decades supports it only in part. Instead, we conclude that disparities in military allocations of goods and burdens sometimes disadvantage racial minorities. This conclusion rests on a review of institutional analyses in five arenas to which researchers have paid close attention: racial patterns in enlistment, officer promotion rates, administration of military justice, risk of death in combat, and health care for wounded soldiers. Although not a direct or intended result of military policy and practice, in three of five cases there was evidence of racial bias and institutional racism. Further work is needed to identify mechanisms through which the bias and racism arose.[11]

14

THE TRANSGENDER VETERAN

Anyone who doubts the lethality of our trans service members should say that to Kristin Beck's face—she's a transgender member of SEAL Team 6, a veteran of Iraq and Afghanistan, and a Bronze Star and Purple Heart recipient.[1]

Representative Sean Patrick (D), New York

The Williams Institute on Sexual Orientation and Gender Identity Law and Public Policy is a public policy research institute based at the UCLA School of Law. They focus primarily on sexual orientation and gender identity issues. In 2014, they came out with a report describing the state of transgenders serving in the U.S. Military: "Our estimates suggest that approximately 15,500 transgender individuals are serving on active duty or in the Guard or Reserve forces. We also estimate that there are an estimated 134,300 transgender individuals who are veterans or are retired from Guard or Reserve service."[2]

Despite these numbers, little research has been conducted in understanding and meeting the needs of the Transgender community.

Although the repeal of DADT [Don't Ask, Don't Tell] was an important step toward addressing the needs of the LBGT* military and veteran population, far more is needed.

Identifying knowledge gaps and novel ways to serve LBGT service members and veterans is imperative. Although the needs of LBGT service members may differ from their non-LBGT peers, little data exists to guide our understanding, and much of what we know is based on

---

* For editorial purposes, LGBT will be used across all resources, rather than LGBTQ or LGBTQI

retrospective studies, veteran reports, and medical record reviews. More research is needed with active duty service members, relying upon novel recruitment strategies that go outside of assessing only those seeking mental and physical health care services. The needs of transgender service members, in particular, demand special attention given the unique experiences this community faces in their interactions with health care providers and the vast disparities faced in numerous mental and physical health diagnoses.[3]

There is general consensus in the medical community that transgender veterans are struggling with mental health issues at a rate higher than the nonmilitary transgender population.

Among military veterans identifying as transgender, 90 percent have at least one mental health diagnosis, such as posttraumatic stress disorder (PTSD) or depression, and nearly 50 percent had a hospitalization after a suicide attempt or suicidal thoughts.

"As more of our active military returns from deployment and transitions to veteran status, the health care system will be faced with treating more transgender veterans who have mental health issues," said principal investigator Marissa Grotzke, MD, an endocrinologist at Salt Lake City Veterans Affairs Medical Center. . . .

Compared with the general U.S. population, the military and its veterans have a fourfold higher rate of gender dysphoria, according to Grotzke. Formerly called gender identity disorder, gender dysphoria is substantial distress associated with nonconformity to one's assigned sex.

Patients with gender dysphoria have unique health care concerns, Grotzke said. In general, they have high rates of depression, anxiety and suicidal thoughts.

Past research also has shown high rates of mental health disorders in military veterans, including PTSD and depression. Less is known, however, about the mental health of veterans with gender dysphoria, she noted.[4]

Tanya Friese served as a Navy Hospital Corpsman in 1991. A number of service-connected medical issues cut short her military career and resulted in her early retirement from the Navy in 1999. Friese completed a bachelor's degree in public health and a master's degree in nursing. She earned her doctorate in nursing practice, which, given her multiple ailments, is quite an achievement.

Friese teaches in the Department of Community, Systems, and Mental Health Nursing at Rush University College of Nursing and is the nursing education manager for extraprofessional continuing education. Her areas of expertise include veterans and their families, individuals with disabilities, and people who identify as LGBT.

Tanya is a great friend. Small and thin in stature, her heart outsizes her small frame. Equally terrific is her wife, Aldonna. My wife and I had the pleasure of attending their wedding a few years back. I am proud to say that I was asked to be a sword bearer for the couple and also proud that, although snug, the military uniform I put down in 2003 still fit! Well, at least the jacket did.

Here is her story.

"I come from a divorced family, where my mom didn't understand the words, 'I love you.' I am thankful for the fact that she did support my decision to join the Navy (despite the 'hissy' fit) and even more grateful that she showed me even greater support when I came back. I was always close to my grandpa—even before I was going to tell him the news, he asked, 'Tanya, do you want to tell me something?'

"In the Navy, I always wanted to fly helicopters. My grandpa always had a special bond with me. 'Tanya, are you going to be a fighter pilot?' he would say. He was very supportive of my dreams, but I was color-blind and could not fulfill this dream.

"For the most part, I enjoyed military life and did well. I mostly kept to myself and worked hard at hiding my sexual identity. I knew that if I was discovered, my career would be over. My identity had to be cloaked like a stealth bomber. I was 'outed' in Germany because people soon realized that I did not have a boyfriend nor did I seem interested in having a boyfriend. It was horrible the way I was treated. I had no support from anyone anywhere. I was alone.

"My service with the Marines* had no problem with my identity and didn't care. I was proud of my service supporting the Marines who, because I was a medic, called me 'Doc,' a huge compliment and honor. They had no problem with my sexual identity, but the Air Force and Navy didn't see things that way.

"I had PTSD and significant gastroenterological problems, and on the basis of that, I sought a medical discharge. The medical board saw nothing wrong with me, so I was headed for a dishonorable discharge because of my identity. But then, I got support from the American Legion, who hired an attorney for me and I got the Honorable Discharge I deserved.

---

* As the Marine Corp has no medical component, they are supported by Navy medical personnel.

"My transition, like most people I suppose, was difficult. But it was magnified because I am a lesbian. I just wasn't prepared for the backlash and it was a totally different situation for me from when I first joined. I turned my attention into achieving what I wanted to do. So I worked at a fertility clinic, which I enjoyed. But I don't like to feel constrained. Never have. So I studied hard, furthered my education, and now I have my doctorate in nursing practice (DNP). But I still suffer physical and emotional pain today."

I asked about how her wife, Aldonna, was handling her return to civilian life.

"My wife is truly a great blessing for me. She is understanding and comforting. At first, the night terrors were horrible as I was reliving some of the death and destruction I had seen. When I would wake up she would grab me violently by the shoulders. 'You're screaming,' she would yell! After two to three years, thanks to treatment and to Aldonna, the night terrors are abating."

"My entire world was based upon the structure and discipline of military service. Sure, I read all the books out there about how to have a successful transition to military life. But, I missed the brotherhood, the comradery, and the 'I got your back' type of responsibility. None of that exists in the states. I never found it in any school or job that I've had.

"I never transitioned. I can't come back. I'm still over there."

I asked, "Do you regret your time in the Navy?"

"No way—I'd go back in a heartbeat," she said.

Rabbah Rona Matlow, MA, ME, is transgender female, an ordained rabbi, and a retired Navy Commander. In her postmilitary life, Rona has had many educational pursuits, including achieving advanced degrees in Jewish education and Jewish studies. In 2003, she entered the Academy for Jewish Religion in New York. She is a freelance therapist that uses social media to reach out to all genders and all veterans. Rona is 100 percent VA certified disabled and her disability income along with her retirement pay gives her the opportunity to help others, mostly free of charge. Perhaps her greatest work is with the Soldiers Project (www.thesoldiersproject.org) and www.translifeline.org. Rona recognizes and appreciates the many life intersections people have. Her counselling is focused on transgender* veterans, but she is open to anyone who needs help.

---

* Cisgender is a term for someone who exclusively identifies as their sex assigned at birth. The term cisgender is not indicative of gender expression, sexual orientation, hormonal makeup, physical anatomy, or how one is perceived in daily life. http://www.transstudent.org/definitions/.

"I enlisted in the United States Navy in April 1979. I was only enlisted for a few years, as I got an ROTC scholarship and was commissioned as a Navy officer in 1982. During my time in service, I worked on nuclear ships and systems management operations.

"During my twenty years of active duty, I didn't identify as transgender, but the signs were always there. At high school, I knew about Renee Richards, Wendy Carlos, and others, but I was never able to put it together to see that I was trans. After I retired, I had a smooth transition home, a better transition than if I had retired in the 1970s.

"We all knew people who were queer. I remember my tour of duty on the USS *Shenandoah* in 1991, which was the first time I worked with women on board. Our group was not so closeted. We all knew if someone [was gay], but we didn't talk about it. Nobody really cared. We all shared bathrooms and workspaces and it just didn't matter. We all worked together to get the job done and people didn't care who you were. Honestly, being Jewish, I received more pressure from proselytizing Christians.

"A large number of queer are atheists. It's not about God, it's about people. I am working with someone who is trans and has been Catholic for two decades. She is very active in her church and community. She sings in the church choir. [But] last week, the priest told her that she is no longer welcome at church. No more choir. No more communion. Go to conversion therapy.

"In 1997, I was working on my first master's in engineering management and had plans to work somewhere in the beltway. I thought I would be forced out in fifteen years, but I made it to twenty. A few years before I left the Navy, I had a huge 'aha' moment.' I was on the wrong path. So I shifted gear and began searching for a new goal. Instead of pursuing engineering, I found it much more meaningful to pursue studies in Jewish education and Jewish studies.

"[Around] 9/11, about a year after I retired, I had plans to be trained as a hospital chaplain and return to the Navy. By that time, I had become involved in the spiritual and emotional side of people. So I started volunteering at the local Disabled Americans Veterans [DAV] office. At DAV, my job was to help process disability claims. Then in 2008, after enduring a long and lingering neck injury earlier in my career, my neck fell apart. By 2010, my neck had degenerated to the point where the VA placed me on medical disability.

"Since I was 100 percent disabled and couldn't be employed full time, all my time was volunteer. Processing claims helped me learn about medicine and psychology and I sort of branched out into becoming a pastoral counselor. Later, I signed up with the Soldiers Project, providing help for vets and families through professional counselling.

"As time wore on, I continued thoughtful self-discovery. Being a voracious reader, I started to learn about the psychological and biological aspects of the cisgender and transgender community. I learned everything I could, including the neurobiology and neuropsychology of PTSD, as well and the intersection with theology. I got credentialed as a certified peer counselor and started providing support for trans and queer. At the same time, I started to realize who I really was. In 2015, I started my physical transitioning in July and came out on Thanksgiving Day.

"Despite all my training and real-life experience, I don't have an of-fice 'shingle.' Because of my disability, I don't work; I volunteer. I'm sort of a freestyle therapist. I don't run clinics, carry no thirty-minute appoint-ments, and have no office staff. I'm just trying to help. I'm lucky because I can maintain financial independence, and I can divide my time locally and across multiple social media sites. Every day someone connects with me, coping with queer things, military things, and I do my best to help them through it.

"Last week, I helped a sixty-five-year-old who is still struggling with PTSD. Yesterday, I was speaking with a fifteen-year-old kid whose parents hate him because he is queer. His parents would rather see him homeless than in their home.

"I've been married for thirty-three years. Although I am transforming to being a trans female, I am still attracted to women. My wife has been with me through all my transitions in life. I believe that too much is made about sexuality. Nobody actually exists in a binary end point of a linear spectrum. Everybody is somewhere in a multidimensional space in both gender and sexuality. You have to be flexible.

"Conventional language would say that I was a straight man and now I'm a lesbian woman. But I'm still the same person I was and still have the same sexuality, so why does the language change? I like terms that take con-ventional terms out of the equation. Those terms just don't work anymore."

Rona and I spent a lot of time addressing the concept of intersec-tionality (which is defined by the *Oxford Dictionary* as "the interconnected nature of social categorizations such as race, class, and gender, regarded as creating overlapping and interdependent systems of discrimination or disadvantage; a theoretical approach based on such a premise").[5] "It's im-portant to understand the concept of intersections of veterans, PTSD, TBI, and queer. PTSD engenders neurobiological changes similar to TBI. It's physical trauma, not psychological trauma. Holding [down] jobs for queer people is very difficult. A large number of queers are oppressed by families, friends, communities, and church. Parents would rather see them dead than queer. Many have experienced sexual molestation as a child. I mean an uncle sees them as less than manly and ends up raping them.

"We all live in a world of complex intersections. Additionally, we have society-based fear: transphobia, transmisogyny, and biases against a number of characteristics in different mixes. When you combine all of these intersections, you come up with someone who is dealing with multiple identities. In my case, I can identify as someone who is Jewish, military veteran, transgender woman, rabbi, counsellor, therapist, 100 percent disabled, and unemployable. Therefore, these characteristics intersect with others who have similar and no similar identities. When you combine all of these things with someone who is queer, you have a much higher level of unemployment, especially if they intersect with also being a woman, black, Hispanic, and so on.

"In general, the person with the most privilege is an abled body white Christian cis hetero binary man. It is the societal ideal. Social disability is a big descriptor of what goes on. Me? All my stuff creates a mess in society. Even before I was transgender, no one wanted to hire me because I was out on disability for so long. They always found some reason as to why they wouldn't hire me.

"Holding jobs is difficult for queers because many have a high degree of social anxiety and an inability to control anger due to lack of social inhibitions. A lot of trans people are on the autism spectrum and that adds another level of complexity to it. In working with queer veterans, you can't just focus on one issue. Concentrating on PTSD and nothing else doesn't work. Most therapy today is another version of whack a mole.

"The trust factor is critical. Take the case of a transgender veteran. If I am counselling them, we don't have to start at zero. We're both trans and we've both worn the uniform. We don't have to take an inordinate amount of time to explain a lot of background that not everybody can [understand]. A doctor might be a great doctor, but not a great doctor for queers. Might be a great doctor, but not a great doctor for a queer veteran. There's a great misogyny center in Philadelphia. Everyone there is queer, so bonds can be built much more quickly."

Cassandra Taylor had a few LGBT friends. "I knew some soldiers who were gay and it really didn't matter to me. It just wasn't that important. This one man asked me to watch *Will and Grace*. So it was subtle things like that where friends can be friends without having an overt conversation about these things.

"There are a lot of homophob[es] in the military. They're hiding. But they want to hurt them. The Army is trying to compare LGBT recognition [in] the same way as black history. You can't compare it. I was born black. I honestly don't believe somebody that is homosexual was born that way. That's my belief and some people don't agree with that. But I don't feel that I have to celebrate that. Me, personally. But if that's your lifestyle. Have at it. I'm not going to hold that against you. If that's how you want to live your life, I will love you and I will embrace you. But I don't have to celebrate the fact that you like someone of the same sexual nature of yourself. I don't. I like a man. Are we going to celebrate 'straight day'? No. So everything is becoming really really crazy so to speak and now people are coming out with it.

"You going to heaven or hell is not going to be based upon me."

Rebecca Solen, who has lived almost all of her life as a man, tells her story.

"I didn't have the words to describe it. I couldn't figure it out. But I knew at the age of five my body was wrong and I grew up with that secret all of my life. Keeping a secret for that long for so long brought on depression, anxiety, and, many times, thoughts of suicide. I was bullied throughout elementary and middle school. To cope, I kept busy in a variety of interests that would push my identity in the background. I got through it because I would distract myself with other things.

"I was always fascinated with the [idea] of serving my country. My dad was a veteran, my grandfather was a veteran, so my family had a line of service. I thought along those same lines. It didn't work out that way initially. I did some missionary work, had a few jobs.

"In 2003 when I finished my bachelor's degree, I asked myself, 'what do I want to do now?' I thought about fulfilling my dream of joining the military and started wondering if this was something that I really wanted to do. In 2003, the war with Iraq was still going on, but I didn't really care too much about that. I did my research and I decided to sign on with the Army because they had a lot of opportunities I was interested in. I went to medic training and became a licensed practical nurse (LPN). Halfway through my training, I had my doubts about becoming an LPN [but] finishing the training. At this time, my depression was kicking in hard and I didn't feel like being an LPN was my best option.

"I had an opportunity to get my commission. In the meantime, I did a brief tour in Germany, only to find out I was accepted for commission. It was a pain, because I had moved the family and kids to Germany, only to come back to the States four months later.

"All this time, I still kept my true identity secret. I was transgender but said nothing to the Army. And no one else either, not my wife, not my family. Nobody.

"My first assignment as a commissioned officer was with the 62nd brigade combat stress control unit at Ft. Lewis, Washington. I was the executive officer. The assignment was excellent. Lots of great caring people, psychiatrists, psychologists, social workers, etc. Lots of people who really care. Not just in the physical sense, but they wanted to help with the mental health well-being of soldiers. I was the only nonclinician on the leadership team. The great part of this assignment was that I had the opportunity to be around these people and to really learn how behavior health works and how salient it is to not just take care of the physical needs of patients, but the mental health needs as well.

"I think that learning about mental health and what makes people tick on the inside influenced me as to how to lead and how to care about people. I learned the compassion of leadership, and as a leader, not to rely on just policy alone. The executive officer is the top administrative position. I was in command and my leadership was not about yelling.

"When necessary, I sat the people under my command down, found out what their motivations were as to why they had made a mistake, and took the time to explain why it was important not to repeat the same mistake. So when punishment was applied, they understood the how and why they did wrong and they truly learned and understood why the discipline was being applied and how they could be better soldiers going forward.

"My next duty assignment was the same position of executive officer at a larger place, Ft. Leonard Wood, Missouri. I enjoyed that assignment, too, but eighteen months in I started to take a hard look at my career, my family, and my wife. We have moved a lot in such a short period of time and I became concerned about my kids. As a military brat, when I was a kid I got tired of moving and losing friends.

"I didn't want my kids to go through that. I was beginning to wonder if a military life is really good for my kids. My fourth child had just been born; my wife was a stay at home mom. When I explained things to my wife why it was time to get out, we prayed, we talked, and we made the best decision.

"So in June 2012, I got out. I wasn't sure what I wanted to do. We settled in to Racine, Wisconsin, where my wife has family. It was a good place to be to get back on our feet. We bought a small house, but I had a hard time finding a job. I took the classes, built my resume, but in Racine few were hiring. I decided to go back to school and I got a degree in information technology. My wife found work with the same company she worked for before I joined the military. For me, after graduation, job recruiters came and I got picked up. Now I have a very good job in information security and digital forensics.

"Something was missing. I still had a strong feeling to contribute to society. I started looking around trying to think where I could make a difference. I found it. In 2015, I started looking at running for office. I've always been a moderate Democrat. Pushed away my identity issues.

"For me, running for Congress was just a way of getting my message out. Money was not the goal and I didn't do many fundraisers. I've always felt that money runs campaigns but votes win elections. I was working full time and trying to be an attentive spouse and taking care of kids; I planned the entire campaign on me just being me. My message resonated with a lot of people. But I didn't get my name out there. I was too busy. I did not have enough opportunity to get my name out.

"I lost the race, but I did get 30 percent of the vote. All of my hard work in the background paid off. The goal I had set, to get out there and run and not necessarily win, had been fulfilled. Besides, winning was not something I could affect—that was for the voters to decide. The things I had learned in the military about leadership and persistence gave me the confidence to put myself out there. I used the experience of being in the military and gained the understanding of who I am, what I can do, and [a willingness to] see just how far I can take things. These skills enabled me to come from nowhere, win the primary, and go up against the third most powerful man in America, Paul Ryan.

"After the election, I made the decision to come out and talk about my true self. My wife was supportive, as well as my family. As you can imagine, this became a big news item. 'Democrat who challenged Paul Ryan comes out as transgender' read the headline. But I am going through with getting the right treatment for me. I have some medical issues, so I won't be running again, but I will continue to serve where I can and hope to champion the rights of transgender people and other issues that are of importance to me."

15

FAMILY IS A CIRCLE
OF STRENGTH

In every conceivable manner, the family is a link to our past, bridge to our future.[1]

—Alex Haley, author

Sgt. 1st Class Kristoffer B. Domeij enlisted a few months before September 11. An Army Ranger, Sgt. Domeij was a Joint Terminal Attack Controller—whose duties included calling in close air support in forward area for ground troops—with Headquarters and Headquarters Company, 2nd Battalion, 75th Ranger Regiment, based at Joint Base Lewis-McChord, Washington. In his ten years of service, Sgt. Domeij was awarded three Bronze Stars and the Purple Heart.

Sgt. Domeij and two other soldiers were killed fighting in the Kandahar province on October 22, 2011. He was twenty-nine years old. He was on his fourteenth deployment.

"To volunteer that many times to deploy speaks volumes to Kris's character and dedication to his country," said Tracy Bailey, spokeswoman for the 75th Ranger Regiment, based at Ft. Benning, Georgia. "He was larger than life. The man everybody wanted to be around."[2]

"In his official Army photo, Domeij looks startled. 'He would have hated that photo, it didn't represent him,' said a friend who called him 'my brother' and submitted an alternate image. 'He was fearless in life and in combat.'

"Domeij had guts but wanted no glory, it seems. Kyle Domeij, of San Diego, said his brother told the family that if anything happened to him, he wouldn't want any media coverage. 'He didn't want to be in the limelight. My brother was a very humble man,' said Domeij. 'We never even knew

all the accomplishments he had. We're just finding out about it now.'"
Domeij is survived by his wife and two daughters.[3]

"Rangers as a whole are quiet professionals and I don't know his rea-
soning behind it, but many Rangers don't see the need to advertise what
they do," Bailey said.[4]

I didn't know Sgt. Domeij. I'm not sure his family knew him either.

Many veterans do not talk about their combat experiences. Not to
their spouses, their families, their friends, and even their therapists. This is
nothing new. A lot of the dads and grandpas from Tom Brokaw's "greatest
generation" never spoke of their experiences either. I've had several people
tell me that the first time they heard about their father's experiences in
World War II was from a battle buddy attending their loved one's funeral.
Then the stories all came pouring out. Stories so valuable that the family
wishes they had heard those stories years ago.

But the veteran couldn't tell.

For many veterans, the experiences are so painful to live with, let
alone explain. Many are convinced that since they are misunderstood in
so many other ways, how could anybody who wasn't there possibility understand what they are feeling right now? Family members try to be supportive, but when the veteran is silent, it is hard for them to understand.

By federal law, the VA cannot treat veterans' family members. Given
the tremendous load and responsibility for treating the millions of veterans
in an essentially socialized medicine environment, I seriously doubt the VA
would be able to add this exponential number of people to their inpatient
and outpatient workloads. Hence, the veterans' treatment, as noble and
advanced as it can be, prohibits the valuable input that families have. As a
parent of a thirty-one-year-old adult son with autism, I can't imagine not
being able to talk to the physician or psychologist as my family and I try
to guide him through life. Home treatment and family is so important in
autism and better outcomes will not happen without family support.

In interviewing veterans transitioning home, I've discovered that they
generally tell me that they want three things: they want the pain to go
away, they want to be left alone, and they want to drink a lot. The most
common response I heard for why the drinking lifestyle was so important
was "so I could sleep." But sleep offered no solace as the night terrors
and flashbacks interrupted sleep—no respite there. Sleep can become an
unwanted and uncontrolled nightmare to the past. When I told my own
psychiatrist I had anxiety and stress when I was sleeping, her response to
me was, "Well, Jaime, we can give you medication to help you through

the day. But your subconscious takes over at night and these drugs can't help you there."

Army Sgt. Dwaine Goings told me his dad owned a liquor store. Instant 24/7 access when he had the keys. Chris Miller said that he became the world's best concealer of bottles. He lived in a tiny apartment and his wife never knew of his drinking problem. Others like Tanya Friese, well, she's convinced that she's never transitioned and she's still back in a warzone.

Still, the ability to carry on and survive learned from extensive training and experience remains, and veterans bring this demeanor to their search for jobs. Coping and survival are strong characteristics of military transition. Even if the family is ready and willing to help, oftentimes they are shut out. They see this downward spiral, yet they are powerless to stop it.

Elizabeth Heaney, MA, LPC, is a counselor who helps service members and their families. She discusses this stress on the family in her book *The Honor Was Mine,*

> Culture shock swings the other way, too. Once a soldier has adjusted to the world of combat, the landscape of home and family can feel foreign and difficult. Accustomed to being immersed in the pressures and clarity of purpose war requires, warriors who have returned home can feel restless, disoriented, frustrated, and distant. The purpose-fueled days of combat, the tight bonds of a tribe of warriors and the sense of pride a soldier feels can all fade away after arriving home. During this transition, such culture-shock symptoms as anger, loneliness, irritation and excessive drinking can arise. The result is emotional turmoil with loved ones—and relationships often crumble.[3]

Dwaine Goings describes how his family was turned upside down when he came home. "All my family was military, but despite this, nobody could reach me. I was acting out and doing all kinds of stupid things. I knew I wasn't right, but I didn't know what to do.

"One night, when I was sleeping, my mom and my sister came into the room. All I saw was these shadowy figures who I knew were coming to kill me. I reached over to my nightstand and got my gun out. Then, I realized who they were and we all breathed a sigh of relief. That was it for that; no more guns around the house for me.

"My wife and I got a divorce because she just couldn't take it anymore. Me getting up at night, yelling and screaming, was just too much. I couldn't sleep. I guess that breaking point was when one night I woke up and I had her in a headlock. That was that!"

Dwaine has four kids, aging in range from their teens to their twenties. I asked him how his relationship with his ex-wife is today. "Sir, *we're the best of friends [laughs].* We talk all the time and everything is as good as it has ever been. We just made the right decision for us and we are both very happy. It's great!" Together, they found a great relationship strategy that works for them. Others are not so fortunate.

Eve B. Carlson, PhD, and Joseph Ruzek, PhD, working at the U.S. Department of Veterans Affairs National Center for PTSD summarize the impact on the family. Carlson breaks it down into several components. It's clear that family often have negative reactions as they watch their loved ones struggle after a deployment.

> Sympathy: One of the first reactions many family members have is sympathy for their loved one. People feel very sorry that someone they care about has had to suffer through a terrifying experience. And they feel sorry when the person continues to suffer from symptoms of PTSD and other trauma responses. . . .
>
> Depression: One source of depression for family members can be the traumatic event itself. All traumas involve events where people suddenly find themselves in danger. When this happens in a situation or place where people are used to feeling safe, just knowing the event happened could cause a person to lose faith in the safety and predictability of life. . . .
>
> Fear and worry: Knowing that something terrible [a flashback, a trigger] can happen "out of the blue" can make people very fearful. This is especially true when a family member feels unsafe and often reminds others about possible dangers. . . .
>
> Avoidance: Just as trauma survivors are often afraid to address what happened to them, family members are frequently fearful of examining the traumatic event as well. Family members may want to avoid talking about the trauma or trauma-related problems, even with friends. [The stigma of mental illness transfers over to them, too.] . . .
>
> Guilt and shame: Family members can feel guilt or shame after a traumatic event for a number of reasons. A family member may experience these feelings if he or she feels responsible for the trauma. . . .
>
> Anger: Anger is a very common problem in families that have survived trauma. Family members may feel angry about the trauma and its effect on their lives [as they may be helpless to deal with a situation they know little about.] . . .
>
> Negative feelings: Sometimes family members have surprisingly negative feelings about the traumatized family member. They may believe the trauma survivor no longer exhibits the qualities that they loved and admired. . . .

Drug and alcohol abuse: Drug and alcohol abuse can become a problem for the families of trauma survivors. Family members may try to escape from bad feelings by using drugs or drinking. A child or spouse may spend time drinking with friends to avoid having to go home and face an angry parent or spouse. . . .

Sleep problems: Sleep can become a problem for family members, especially when it is a problem for the trauma survivor. When the trauma survivor stays up late to avoid going to sleep, can't get to sleep, tosses and turns in his or her sleep, or has nightmares, it is difficult for family members to sleep well. . . .

Health problems: Family members of trauma survivors can develop health problems for a number of reasons. Bad habits, such as drinking, smoking, and not exercising may worsen as a result of coping with a loved one's trauma responses.[6]

Michael Brennan from the Road Home Program offers his experience in working with patients and families. "The hardest thing for the family is that [they think] now that their love one comes home, we're going to pick up where we left off. And it doesn't happen. War changes people. Injuries change people. And the families have changed. They may not realize it, but during the deployment, they, too, have moved in a different way and perhaps moved on to different things. At the end of the day, I think the hardest lesson to learn is that sometimes love is not enough. They think that if they love this person enough, that is going to be the thing that will fix them. Love is necessary, but not sufficient. You need to have that care for the vet, but the vet also needs other things to get better. The family needs other things to get better. Helping families build a whole new way of working with a whole new set of skills that they need to help this vet. So you treat the veteran on one hand, with evidence based treatments that you know are going to help them improve their PTSD symptom or improve their TBI, and then give the family some skills, and they kind of come back together again."

One of the key success stories for the Road Home Program has been the integration of families into the healing process, something the VA cannot do because they do not have the authorization from the federal government to provide such services. I asked Dr. Mark Pollack, medical director of the Road Home Program, to comment on the family aspects of veteran healing.

"In order to treat the very complex challenges veterans face, the Road Home Program realizes the power and the value of family involvement. We incorporate the family into our evidence based treatment strategies by offering an array of family services, including psychotherapy, spouse involvement and support, couples therapy, and other social services.

"Our family therapy and support services help rebuild relationships. Trust can never be assumed. We do intensive treatments in groups, whether it's veterans connecting with other veterans or veterans healing with their families. We established an intensive three-week outpatient program for the veteran where the relationship is repaired and healing begins. During the third week, we fly out the veteran's family members to participate in psychotherapy.

"Through this group therapy approach we are able to reduce the effects of the invisible wounds of war. We concentrate on overall health and well-being strategies including exercise and other stress reducing activities. Group therapy also helps us specialize in specific therapies that target the critical and specific needs of each and every veteran. And we enjoy working with other community agencies to keep a pulse on what needs are out there and how together we can keep a pulse on what is working and what other treatments are out there that can be used in our program."

Will Beiersdorf, executive director of the Road Home Program, talks about his personal experience as well as strategies and tools his program uses to integrate and include family members into the treatment process.

"As a vet, returning from deployment changed everybody's lives and laid a new sense of trauma and anxiety in everybody. For me, I saw the attacks on 9/11 and I think it changed all of us. These men and women are asked to do things in challenging situations.

"When I came back from Cuba, I had difficulty explaining things. I would say: 'Don't you understand there's some sense of urgency here?? We are at war here.' Not everybody was on board and less than 1 percent served.*

"There are things that have happened to these people and the Road Home Program plays a vital role in helping and providing the tools for a pathway forward. Working with the VA and other agencies is salient as there is no one that can work in isolation in helping these veterans.

"When the conflict started, I fully comprehended the impact: these men and women were being ground up. That's the real challenge of this generation; you're fighting an enemy, you're fighting an ideology that is invisible. The enemy uses tools to terrorize that damage us physically and internally.

"Families are deeply affected by these deployments. We finally have taken the cloak off of this. In the past, we've been in conflicts where you start here and end there. We've really never been in a conflict that has no

---

★ Of the U.S. population.

end. And I think people don't realize this. So the constant activations and constant deployments are taking a toll on these families, including the psychiatric needs of the children as they kind of act out things.

"Even for myself, after being gone for less than a year in Guantanamo Bay, I still think to this day that my youngest of three sons . . . my youngest son had the most separation anxiety. I mean the kid was constantly on me, so afraid that I would leave. Even to this day, if I go somewhere, he'll say, 'hey, Dad, when are you coming back'; whereas my other two boys couldn't care less. Even from normal service, you come back different. But now you have this changing during a war. When these men and women come back they try to relate."

Retired Army Colonel Charles W. Hoge writes in his book *Once a Warrior, Always a Warrior:*

> Everyone grows, matures and changes during the absence. Spouses and partners become much more independent. Children may reach major milestones (e.g. walking, talking). Young children may not remember the warrior, or may have difficulty adjusting to new routines, shared custody or a move when the warrior returns. Role changes in the household can be challenging. Warriors may have a hard time transferring responsibilities to their spouse/partner and then on return unrealistically expect that the roles should go back to the way they were before deployment.[7]

Will goes on to talk about specific tools and strategies that are used by the Road Home Program. "Critical tools are needed and given to the family as they are with the vet in the morning when everybody gets up and there when everyone goes to bed at night. Giving them the tools and ability, not just to try to understand what the veteran is going through, but also to help give the veteran a sense of purpose. Love is a big component, but the veteran needs some purpose.

"Show your love but continue to show them their purpose. Step by step give them responsibility so they don't try to insulate themselves. A lot of these vets don't know they have a problem, until they hit rock bottom. Our program helps them do that.

"Encourage them to be open about the family member being deployed. This can be counterintuitive for families who say 'Don't need help. We got this.' Even in my circumstance, my neighbors started to ask, 'Where's Will?' 'Oh, he's deployed.' So, it's like fifteen years in the village and nobody knew I was in the Reserves.

Ivan Vasquez is in the EN-Abled Vet Internship. He met all the requirements to be entered in the Epic Systems ambulatory class and is doing very well as of this writing. With that Epic Certification, starting salaries often start around the $60,000, with potential for much more. He has a bright future and a solid family around him.

But that was not always the case. I interviewed his wife, Janet, to get her perspective on Ivan's military service and the impact it had on the Vasquez family.

"When Ivan came back it was really tough for him. He was going deeper and deeper into depression. He felt really bad that without a job, he was not providing for his family. It was a very difficult time for us. I know he had it much worse than us, even if I didn't know all the details. I tried to tell him to give it a little time, but he was in a bad place.

"Ivan went on two deployments: one to Iraq and one to Afghanistan. When he came back, he was different. He was very strict and very quiet, which I understand from what I know about his deployment. While he was gone, I went to family counselling, which was helpful. They told me, 'Whatever you do, don't ask what happened over there. If he wants to tell you, he will tell you. When he's ready to talk, be there for him. If he doesn't talk about it, then just let it go.' So that's what I did.

"One night we went out dancing. There were a lot of people there from different cultures. We were having a good time. Then, all of a sudden, he grabbed me and held me really tight. I asked if anything was wrong, and he said, 'Don't you know what today is? It's September 21st.' I did what I usually do and that is to try to talk him down from whatever anxiety is bothering him. I said, 'What's so special about September 21st?' Something hit him and he snapped at me and said, 'You don't understand. A year ago today, I was working out when bombs started hitting the gymnasium. I thought for sure I was going to die. All I could think about was you, the kids, and my mom. I thought this was it and that I would never see you ever again.' I started crying and we both left dancing quickly and came home.

"I work nights to support our family, including Ivan and our two teenage daughters—now and when Ivan was away. Ivan was feeling useless. I made the right connection with him when I told him that even though he wasn't working, he was helping me a lot. He was helping our daughters with homework, he was cleaning and taking care of the household, which, I told him, I greatly appreciated because it was taking a lot of burden off of me.

"We were doing OK for a while, but after talking to some of his old buddies, Ivan began looking for deployments he could go on. Ivan was told that a group was deploying to Egypt real soon. He wanted to go back so badly. This would often come up when he got rejected for jobs. 'This is not me,' he would say. 'This is not my life.' I would tell him, 'Ivan, you have a family that needs you. We want to keep moving forward with our lives. We want to keep going. I support you as much as I can, but you have to help us. He would say, 'I know. But every time I get rejected for a job, I want to go back.' 'Don't leave us. Don't give up.'

"My daughter took these deployments hard. She would say, 'I have no dad and mom is always working.' She would say, 'I'm going to perform at an assembly and my dad is the only dad not here. I want my dad to be proud of me, but he's not there.' To hear these things broke my heart. Ivan missed a lot of things like holidays and birthdays.

"While Ivan was gone, I turned to his mom for support and she turned right back to me for support. We never had a bad relationship, but when Ivan was gone, she, too, was taking the deployment really hard. Some nights, we would get together and just cry. Sometimes it was my turn, other times it was hers.

"Things turned for the better when Ivan found his place with the EN-Abled Veteran Internship. He got so excited and he told me, 'Janet, I'm going to have to study really hard. This is really important. This is my future. I will make maybe $60,000 when I get my certificate. This EN-Abled Veteran Internship is the thing I've been looking for.

"Finally, Ivan started to feel good about himself. It's very important for Ivan to feel like he is making contributions to the family. He found the sense of purpose he was looking for. Today our outlook is bright. Ivan is going to pass his tests and be very successful. It makes our family feel good. Sometimes, he'll share a little bit of what it was like to be over there, but those moments are less and less and I feel comfortable that he has told me just about everything.

"My advice to families who are reading this is to try to support your husband or wife as much support as you can. Find things for them to do to contribute to the family. Be patient and they will find their purpose. Always be supportive and remember, don't push it. If they want to talk, they will talk. Most of the time, just being there will make a big difference."

16

BEING ALL IN

If people are going to judge me without fully understanding the content of my character, then their opinion just isn't worth it.[1]

—Jazz Jennings, American activist

In World War II, combat units were overwhelmingly white. As far as the average American was concerned, World War II was a white man's war.[2] There was an enlisted group of Japanese Americans who fought in Europe. American Indians worked in code talking.[3] Some 350,000 women served mostly in traditional roles of the time.[4] Little is known about transgenders in World War II, probably because they hid their self-identity from others, a practice that continues today.

The military did not integrate until President Truman issued an executive order to do so, in 1948, three years after the war ended.[5] When the United States needed it most, minority groups proved their value to the country. Seventy years later, despite proving value time after time, there still is divisiveness.

The voices in this book, from the veterans who served and those that support them, bring forward a melting pot of social issues, many of which we never talk about. There were pockets of racism and sexism among the ranks. Rona works with transgenders who battle external and internal anxieties. Cassandra stated unequivocally that racism was everywhere. Dwaine was arrested by two white police officers who didn't understand his PTSD. Tanji, Bea, and Dee saw no discrimination but acknowledge that it probably did exist. When Tanji returned home after five years overseas, she asked her friends, "You still have that race problem over here?"

131

Similar pockets of equality and inequality exist in America today. Given the tightness of some service units, it's not surprising to hear that some minorities didn't feel the sting of prejudice. What a person believes and what their identity is becomes irrelevant when you are counting on that someone to save your life.

Approximately one hundred and fifty thousand individuals who identify as transgender have served or are serving in the active duty, guard, and reserve forces.[6] Transgender military members are still fighting for their country and for equality in the military. One president promotes transgender inclusion. The next one says transgender military personnel cost too much. Such reversals confuse all able-bodied Americans who wish to fight for our freedom.

We found that a different identity is not something easily seen; it's possible to hide. But you have to be really good at it, like Rebecca. Who can imagine holding in that secret for almost all of her life? From everyone. And what a powerful stigma to force her to have to feel that hiding it is not an option. Tanya has overcome enormous military hate and now she has to deal with rejection from the healthcare community when she needs it most.

But we also have the voice of an older Muslim man loving a young Christian man. We heard the voice of a Muslim man who spoke of hugging a Jewish man. We heard the voice of a woman from a former Eastern Bloc country accepted to the point where her PTSD has been significantly reduced. We saw a workforce transformed just by accepting and embracing the differences of others. Finding common ground. Connecting at the very root of human existence.

Wars are fought as a reflection of the culture in which they exist. This statement is simplistic, prolific, and, admittedly, obvious. Centuries of war have happened without an airplane, battleship, automatic weapon, or hand grenade. Yet common threads remain: culture, political will, ideology, and leadership to name a few. They directly impact strategy and operations at all levels.

Today's wars are like no others in world history. Technology has changed our lives at breakneck speed, with no sign of abatement. With such a cultural and generational shift, wars are now using new technologies to gain political advantage but also to kill people. The differences in the wars we fight today are as profound as the differences between Pearl Harbor and the World Trade Center.

The United States doesn't fight enemy countries as in years past. Over two hundred thousand people were killed during the bombings of Hiroshima and Nagasaki, effectively ending World War II.[7] Many of these casualties were civilians. Social conscience for civilians was not a major issue.

It wasn't until the Viet Nam War that we began to really think about sparing civilians. For the first time, videos from the day or previous day were readily available on the evening news. Previously, no one had seen too much war coverage unless they went to the movies where, minus television, heavily edited visuals of the war were seen.

Today's wars are fought with "surgical strikes" of "military targets." Civilian deaths are instantly broadcast. Free world military leaders are vilified for civilian casualties, yet brutal dictators, not so much. Those that do us harm do not look for military targets. They look for public places, such as churches, malls, movie theaters, and shopping centers where there are nothing but civilians. These are places where suicide bombers strike.

As part of our defensive strategy, the United States takes enormous steps to prevent other countries from developing the same weaponry that we possess, while continuing to build more capabilities. Remember the Reagan-era space-based weapons strategy referred to as "Star Wars"? How about advancing technology to support an arms race? Even when real war wasn't happening, we made up a new war and called it the Cold War.

The United States continues to invest billions of dollars trying to stop the proliferation of weaponry that we ourselves have created. North Korea's capability of delivering a nuclear bomb to our shores has become a grave concern for America over the last ten years. Thankfully, the United States turns to another type of war, but the weaponry is "economic sanctions," which can be quite punishing and doesn't involve firing a single shot.

Egregious as war is, if you turn on your television these days, you may get the impression that the United States likes war. We are polarized, politically and culturally. We are now in our seventeenth year of fighting with Afghanistan, and although the mission of removing the Taliban during the first month was met, the U.S. military is still there. Yet there is fighting in our streets at home. You may be surprised to learn that there were 149 U.S. Special Operations Forces deployed in 2017.[8] Drones constantly scan for both defensive and offensive purposes. War is everywhere, and we pay a price for being the world's police force.

There is one type of war, however, that the United States is not used to fighting, and that is the religious war or Holy War. From the Crusades of the eleventh century, to the tension between the Sunnis and the Shiites today, Holy Wars have been fought for centuries. But the United States is less than 250 years old and does not share that history. A Holy War is a war that we do not fully comprehend as the United States has never really been involved in this type of war and grapples with how to fight it.

The United States fights for freedom and democracy and the American way (just like Superman). But the American way may not reflect the way of another culture or religion and the values imposed by the United States might not be accepted.

The United States fought for freedom in Iraq, but were the Iraqi people involved in what this definition of freedom means? Did we fight for freedom, or did we fight to destroy a perceived cache with weapons of mass destruction? Would we have even gone there if we knew that fracking would make the United States the world's largest producer of oil in the world?

These aspects of war—culture, ideology, religion, and technology— influence the performance and behavior of a new type of American soldier, sailor, airman, and marine. Culture permeates our branches of service: the way they think, act, and fight. And it will continue to be that way. No high school graduate knows life before 9/11. Soon, no college graduate will know of life pre-9/11 as well.

Three questions that need to be asked when considering armed conflict are: What are we doing, why are we doing it, and how do we make things better? For World War II: We were fighting to defeat Germany and Japan. We were fighting because we were attacked and we needed to support our allies. We made things better by stopping fascism across the globe. Today, we are fighting foreign and domestic terrorism. We are doing this to keep America safe. We make things better by stopping terrorism across the globe. Yet Congress had not declared war in almost eighty years.

Stopping terrorism is difficult to achieve. Perhaps this explains why the war in Afghanistan is dragging on with no end in sight. Who can defeat an army of one with a bomb strapped to his or her chest?

Complicating the landscape is the fact that wars are no longer something happening "over there." Terrorists are bringing the war to our streets, our schools, our public places. To fight these wars, we have been vigilant in our behavior and shoeless before boarding an airplane.

The United States struggles to embrace diversity, yet it is quick to point out failures with political correctness. A tweet or a post can change American policy. Sometimes social media is more dangerous than helpful. Warren Buffet once said that it takes twenty years to build a reputation and five minutes to ruin it.[9] Social media tools such as texting, Twitter, and instant messaging have amplified that.

Finally, there is a new type of war that the world is just beginning to embrace, cyberwarfare. This warfare has dismantled or hacked networks at banks, hospitals, and even presidential elections. Resources that were protected by concrete and barbed wire are now being compromised. This new weapon may or may not be sponsored by countries; the enemy may be simply rogue individuals. Cyberwarfare gives weaponry to teenagers on a laptop, sitting at home in their bedrooms.

All of these shifts affect the spectrum of the American warfighter: motivation, confidence, morale, support, and treatment. Older methods for equipping, training, supporting, and treating are no longer adequate. Despite all this, with agility the military still does a tremendous job of preparing the military for war and treating the injuries associated with war.

At the same time, military members are inadequately prepared for the return home. This was demonstrated by the interviews conducted for this book and the statistics supplied from numerous studies. GI Joe finds that the deployment to the warzone was easier than the transition back home. The social fabric is on a different path. Not only does the old road no longer exist, but it was a crummy road to begin with.

Evidence based practice in creating a new path has paved the way for new thoughts and ideas in treating veterans. These new ideas work. They expose the invisible wounds and offer veterans treatments that nobody had thought of before. Take exposure therapy. For decades, the veteran was given counselling and medications because that's what the medical field knew and what doctors had been taught. Today we have more technology and tools to help veterans. But socially and operationally, it's time to build new bridges for coming home.

Coping is one of the biggest challenges for our military veterans. The coping skills mastered overseas are different than the ones needed back home. Veterans went to a new normal when they deployed, but going back to the old normal may not be possible. Coping with home and the way the changed veteran now thinks can be extremely difficult.

From battle fatigue to PTSD, alcohol remains the number one mental health treatment of choice, aka problem, for many veterans. Why not? It's relatively cheap, easy to get, works quickly, doesn't require a prescription, makes for a great sleeping pill, and substitutes for a lot of friends. But what happens the morning after? Do the same thing? Clearly, alcohol is not the answer and creates more problems than it solves.

Then there's suicide. According to the Department of Veterans Affairs, twenty veterans commit suicide every day.[10] The accuracy of this figure is somewhat controversial. Some experts think it's not that high; others think it may be too low. After all, how many inexplicable high-speed single car or motorcycle deaths occur each day? As Dr. Karnic told me,

"We know the suicide probability rate is high for those that have made at least one attempt. But I worry about those that don't come in to the Road Home Program at all."

One of the most enduring problems for military veterans, for the last one hundred years, is the loss of a sense of purpose. Many Americans experience this every single day. Feelings of failure appear all too soon. Let's not forget anxiety and depression for those of us who have lost jobs and perhaps have had to switch careers.

The sense of despair heightens when the days of unemployment begin to stack up. This argle-bargle option for veterans become impossible to maneuver. Veterans have told me that they were led to believe that society would take them back with open arms and jobs for veterans were plentiful. I was lucky. My healthcare job was similar to healthcare IT in the civilian sector. Tommy Bankhead and others also had easy transitions.

Coming home for veterans is difficult and it becomes more complicated when some of what they were promised is simply not true. Yes, they get healthcare, but they might have to wait a month. Yes, they can apply for disability benefits, but they might have to wait years.

There are many well-meaning companies that have stepped forward and said, "We will hire veterans" or "No veteran will be turned away." But what is the quality of these jobs and do they match the depth and breadth of what the military person has been doing for four years or longer?

There are some veterans who might be happy with menial, unskilled jobs that pay close to minimum wage. But others, particularly those who had enormous responsibility in their military careers, have the strong desire to give back. Some have become teachers, police officers, and firefighters.

Some companies practice a "fake out" to strengthen their brand and give the illusion of helping veterans. A couple of years ago, I had the opportunity to speak to a vice president at a prominent U.S. bank. "Jaime, we've started a brand-new website just for veterans."

"Great," I said. "How does it work?"

"Well," he stated, "veterans can log on to a site just for them and apply directly for open jobs at our bank."

"So what is the difference between your regular site and the one that the veterans use?" I asked.

"Well, when somebody applies on our veterans website, an actual human will look at the resume, rather than automatically being screened out by our sophisticated recruitment software."

"I see. Then what happens?" I asked. "Do you take it a step further, or do you toss it in the bin?"

"Well, um. We look at it, but yes, a lot of these don't go much further. Jaime, these resumes are just not very well written."

Great.

There was another time when a large nonprofit group called me and said, "Hey, we want to make veterans a major focus next year. Could you help us?"

"Absolutely," I said, getting excited. "How about at your next major conference, we put a program or workshop together that can really get the word out and help some veterans?"

"Oh, we didn't quite have that in mind," was the response. "We were thinking about having you do a couple of webinars in about eight months from now. Are you still interested?"

"Sure," I said, totally deflated. I can't wait nine months and neither can many veterans.

I get a fair number of these offers. I call them pretenders, rather than contenders. It's not necessarily that those making the offers are bad people, but they are people who are misinformed about what it's like to come home from war and start over. Some companies say they want to help, but they only want to scrape the surface, and don't truly understand that veterans aren't used to networking, resumes, and job interviews. Then there are those who use returning veterans as part of a marketing strategy. This often gets me discouraged, especially when I see that bank waving the flag in a television commercial promoting opportunities for veterans I know from personal experience do not exist.

There's a gap that many people don't understand. One big gap is communication. I have had several veterans come to me and say, "Y'know what, Jaime? I put a lot of work into my research and preparation. I must have sent my resume to twenty different websites and companies. I would check my email ten times an hour for a week. And you know what? Not one of them ever contacted me. I don't think they like veterans."

"Welcome to your new normal, son," was my response. "They're not going to contact you. They get thousands of resumes and don't often give feedback." Most veterans are stunned when they hear this. The formula is apply for a job, get the job, or get some sort of thank you for playing. Maybe this is how your dad got a job, but it doesn't work that way anymore. Most job seekers know this, but for veterans who never had to compete for jobs, this is a startling revelation. If you weren't aware of the twenty-first-century job seeking change in the game, how would you know?

One person who is definitely a contender is Judy Faulkner, founder and CEO of Epic Systems. Epic is the largest and best electronic medical record software company out there, in my opinion. When I approached Judy at a conference with the EN-Abled Vet Internship concept, she jumped on board. Together, we constructed a program that gave veterans an opportunity for Epic certification. Three years later, over fifty veterans from twelve different states and fifteen different specialties have gained certification. Because of the popularity of Epic and the need for analysts, salaries start around $60,000/yr. Not just the start of a job, but the start of a healthcare IT career.

I asked my Epic colleagues for the names of these healthcare systems [where the vets were working], but they refused, citing privacy issues. I told them I just wanted to call and thank the CIOs who made this happen, but they held firm. Needless to say, I was not very pleased, yet their concerns were well founded.

Then I paused . . . wait a minute. In less than three years, the EN-Abled Veteran Internship had expanded across the United States. The fact that I didn't know where was inconsequential. Instead, it was kind of cool. With Judy's help, the planning that she and I had done gave careers to faceless veterans whose names I will never know. And that is just fine with me.

I'm proud of all veterans, some of whom have come back from incredible odds to get jobs and careers in healthcare IT. One vet I'm particularly fond of is Kevin Gonzalez, a twenty-three-year-old Marine who was broke, desperate, and on the verge of homelessness. Kevin was our first veteran to get Epic Ambulatory Certification and he landed a job at Centura Health in Denver, Colorado. His starting salary was $62,000/yr. Amy Feaster, vice president of information technology at Centura Health in Colorado, was so impressed with Kevin that she started her own EN-Abled Veteran Internship.

When Kevin got the job, this lachrymose Marine came into my office one day and told me, "Jaime, my father never made more than $30,000/yr. his entire life. Now here I am, at age twenty-three, on my way to Colorado with at $62,000/yr. job. I can't even begin to thank you."

"You just did," I told him.

The EN-Abled Veteran Internship has been adopted by other health systems, but not all of them have been successful. One healthcare system created a veteran's council and was really excited about the program. When I called my contact for the program, he told me the program had folded.

"What happened?" I asked.

"Well, we got off to a good start. We had two very strong candidates and they were doing well. But they wanted jobs here and we didn't have any for them. They knew this going in, but got bitter and angry anyway. They ended up leaving the program early."

"What about the council?" I asked.

"We disbanded. Of the six members, I was the only veteran. People got busy, stopped going to the meetings, and it all kind of fizzled out."

"Do you still keep in touch with the veterans?"

"No," he said. "We did end up having two openings after they left, however."

"Did you call them?" I asked.

"No," he said.

"Why not?"

"Well, we figured that if they wanted to work here they'd keep watching and stay in touch. But because they disengaged, we thought they didn't care. We were looking for a little more initiative, quite frankly," he concluded.

Again, a cultural gap that causes a miscommunication gap.

Obviously, I was crushed to hear this, but like most things you try for the first time, I learned something. Starting a program like this does take an investment. There were plenty of days where the clouds were dark and the energy was thin. But we kept the passion going, worked at it, and it paid off.

To successfully hire a veteran, you have to create an environment where they are comfortable and your staff is comfortable. There is more freedom in the civilian world: competitive pay, fewer restriction on dress and haircuts, and more autonomy in making decisions and career changes. Having veterans on your staff to meet, greet, and orient new veteran hires gives a huge lift for new veteran employees. They gain confidence that they will be understood and can integrate into the job environment.

If you're going to help a veteran, you must be all in. If you're hiring a veteran because you feel sorry for them or you're looking for a tax break, you are hiring a veteran for the wrong reasons. You see, it's not about you, it's about them.

We went into this program with the concept that we were giving vets a skill, which we were. But so much more happened. Remember Bea stating that EN-Abled Veteran Internship cured her PTSD? Didn't see that coming. Remember Tommy discussing the importance of trust and acceptance? How about the multicultural hugs from Karim, Ryan, and Sid? One veteran got a job selling insurance annuities.

"How did that happen?" I asked him.

"Well, I used to sell annuities about fifteen years ago. I learned a little about information technology, but what the program did for me was give me confidence that I could 'fit in' and be accepted by others. So they are going to send me to six weeks of paid training, and I'll be full time and up-to-date with today's annuities." Didn't see that coming. Here I was thinking we were training for IT careers and someone comes along and says that we were training him to reintegrate into the civilian workforce.

Then there's Willie Mayers. If that names sounds familiar, well, his dad was a big fan of Baseball Hall of Famer Willie Mays, so he named his son Willie. Willie was one of the sweetest guys to come into our program. Soft-spoken, pleasant, and reassuring—everybody fell in love with Willie. I'm guessing but I think Willie was a little over 6 feet tall and on a good day, probably weighed about 115 lbs. His terrific wife was about four inches shorter and twenty pounds lighter. They are a wonderful and beautiful couple.

We took our time with Willie and the staff simply embraced this man. Talking to Willie was kind of like talking to a stately gentleman from the late 1800s. Just a joy to be around. Needless to say, he sailed through the mock job interview process. Willie got picked up by a construction company doing customer service calls. We were all thrilled and consumed with joy when he got the job offer. We were sad to see him go but so proud of him regardless.

Oh, I forgot to mention a couple of things. Willie left the military over thirty years ago, and he had just recently celebrated his sixty-eighth birthday. Success!

Finding a job in the direct patient care world can be extremely frustrating. Researchers from the University of Washington recently conducted a survey to assess the challenges for veterans bringing medical skills learned in the military to the civilian world: "Four thematic areas emerged from the literature on the barriers that veterans face when attaining a healthcare career: 1) navigating complex benefits, 2) translating military education and training to civilian occupations, 3) meeting credentialing requirements, and 4) overcoming limited communication and knowledge about healthcare career opportunities."[11] These veterans fought in intense combat zones and probably saw more trauma in four years than a direct care worker sees in twenty. Yet they are denied certification because they don't have a degree, or in one case I know of, needed twelve credit hours in algebra, English, history, and a foreign language of their choosing. I can go with an emergency medical technician who worked in a combat zone not knowing the Pythagorean theory.

Being all in is not all about jobs, it includes veterans' health, too. On the clinical side, one of the many strengths of the Road Home Program is its ability to incorporate families into the therapy sessions. Sometimes families are the last hope for some veterans. Who saved Dwaine Goings? His mom, of course. Who turned Chris Miller away from suicide? His wife.

You may not always be able to rely on buddies and comradery to get you through the tough times. Often, their struggles may be similar to yours. Some vets like Chris don't want to ever see their buddies; it brings the war closer in the rearview mirror.

Evidence based practice works. These techniques are not unique to veterans; these tools are used throughout the spectrum of medicine, and often in psychiatry. New research has led practitioners to try new treatment techniques. Some have worked; others have not.

It would seem unimaginable a few decades ago that exposing veterans to the horrors of war, rather than the well-accepted practice of counselling and pills, would be effective. But that's just how exposure therapy works. With realistic virtual reality technology, veterans directly confront what happened to them rather than trying to bury it. But the challenge remains for adequate physician training. Since physicians interrupt their patients on average every eleven seconds, it is imperative, not to mention their responsibility, that doctors be open to new treatment modalities. It's just difficult to do in a fifteen-minute appointment.[12]

There are exciting new technologies that are helping to expand the delivery model of care. The VA has announced its expansion of telemedicine, where video visits can reach out to veterans who live in rural areas. Such technology can reach veterans anywhere in the country.[13]

Perhaps as the VA continues to move forward with the enormous task in front of them, they will be allowed to work with families directly, integrating the whole family to help the whole person. Regardless, you have the power to be an eucatastrophe to veterans coming home.

As the programs at Rush gained momentum, a lot of people came to me with compliments, but more important, asking for ways they could help. When I queried them as to what they would like to do, I received a lot of interesting answers but a common theme. It seems that many people are searching for a way to help their fellow human beings but don't quite know how. We live in a very busy world. The technology that was designed to make our lives better has somehow just made our lives busier. In the 1960s, we "dropped out"; today, we "go off the grid."

Helping veterans is relatively easy; it takes minimal effort to find them and they are so easy to find. There are over seven thousand not-for-profit organizations supporting veterans today.[14] Find one that meets your own company's culture and get involved. While donations are always nice, the EN-Abled Veteran Internship and Road Home programs thrive on the personal interactions of people. Don't be afraid of the power of diversity. Bias and fear melt away. Consciousness, understanding, and appreciation grow.

17

I, VETERAN

Sometimes people think they know you. They know a few facts about you, and they piece you together in a way that makes sense to them. And if you don't know yourself very well, you might even believe that they are right. But the truth is, that isn't you. That isn't you at all.[1]

—Leila Sales, American author

I am the twenty-first-century veteran. Like my brothers and sisters from previous wars, I share a common bond in preserving the freedoms and liberties all Americans enjoy. I did what I did and I do what I do because I, too, felt the strong patriotic bonds of those that came before me. I am proud to have served and will challenge those that threaten my core values as they relate to the nation I served and those with whom I served.

Yet I am who I am. I come from a generation dramatically different from those before me. I have grown up in a digital world, with access to information and technology never dreamed of in previous generations. I have also fought wars more digital in nature, with advance weaponry and communications. It doesn't matter. My brothers and sisters died in my arms just as in previous generations, but because of the cultural differences, I am different and so are you.

Here are ten things I want you to know about me. They are important for me to know and equally important for me to tell you. For the better understanding we have between us, the more accepting and comfortable you will be of me and the more comfortable and accepting I will be of you.

My older veteran brethren see these differences and understand, but the average American may not have this insight.

1. I am as patriotic as any America has ever been.

I got really angry and energized at 9/11. You did too, but I went and put it all out there. I may have been a little naïve and thought it was one big video game, but I went anyway. I want to kill these guys that did this to our country. Sign me up, right now! I'm all in.

I am proud to have served, visited some amazing places, and made some amazing friends. These experiences have changed me, but for the most part I think it has been for the better. But I understand that some of those that served with me may have been hurt. These people need help, but I look at my friends and it seems to me that they may not be getting the help they deserve. I got a half dozen buddies that never made it back. Man, we put it all out there for Uncle Sugar. Where is he now?

2. My military experience was unique to me and me alone.

Some of us experienced combat and some of us didn't. Some of us experienced prejudice and harassment while in uniform, some of us didn't. A one-size-fits-all veteran doesn't really exist, so try not to make too many assumptions about me. I may have been deployed or never saw combat, but I still may suffer from PTSD or MST. Don't assume that because I may be a Marine in a combat area that I shot somebody. Don't ever ask me what it's like to kill somebody. I probably wouldn't tell you anyway.

I'm getting sick and tired of the "thank you for your service." You know how many times I've heard that? It doesn't mean anything to me. Better to say "never forget." It makes me realize that you understand that we are all in this together. You want to thank me for my service? How about giving me a job? How about giving me an appointment at the VA? How about trying to understand me?

3. I'm coming home from a war I didn't win.

I served. I did my best. I came home but my buddies may still be over there. I may have gotten a parade and other types of recognition, but the war continues with no end in sight. I think about going back sometimes. Sometimes, it may be all I think about, especially if I'm sitting at home with a lot of idle time on my hands.

I can't believe some of the things I see on TV. We fought and died over there and now I see all that territory is being lost again. Why can't we finish this thing? Did I waste my time over there? Did my friends die for nothing?

4. I may have invisible wounds not seen in other wars.

Because of advances in battlefield triage, transportation, and advanced surgical care, many of my military battle buddies survived their wounds. The enemy also uses more nonconventional weaponry such as roadside bombs, suicide bombers, and close action combat. Battle buddies who would have died in previous wars are being saved, but they are coming home with missing limbs, PTSD, or TBI. The number of these veterans is much higher than in previous wars. Because of the complexities of these types of injuries, these veterans may need care for the next fifty to sixty years.

You may never know about my internal struggles. Many of us suffer in silence, just like other veterans from other wars. There are advanced treatments out there that I may or may not be open to. It's not your fault if I cannot communicate these things to you. I need help but I may not know how to get it. I may need to hit rock bottom first.

Some veterans cannot be reached and this is gut wrenching to all of those around. I see it. Some veterans cannot be saved. The suicide rate for us is upward of twenty per day and that doesn't count those of us who drive headfirst into a tree. I don't have any easy answers except to say keep trying and don't give up on us, even when we give up on ourselves.

5. I need a job sooner rather than later.

While the new benefit programs that have been established and the opportunities for veterans from the large number of not-for-profits have increased, please remember one thing: I'm not out of the service; I'm cash strapped, and my income is gone. Perhaps I should have planned better for this, but maybe I never got around to it. You don't get rich in the military and now that the income is gone, I need help.

I'm glad I have the opportunity to get an education, and I appreciate the many programs that help to keep me off the streets, but I need a job. And I'm not quite sure how to get one. I might not be able to wait two to four years to get a degree; I need to put food on the table. It's worse for me if I'm going through a divorce or have children to support. I'm not used to money not coming in twice a month as it did on active duty. Maybe I lived in base housing all my career and have never had to apply for rent or a mortgage. Maybe my credit score is low.

But I need to work.

6. Something has got to restore my sense of purpose.

Y'know what? I was da bomb in the military. I was it! Everyone counted on me. If I didn't get it done bad things happened. I was in charge of five hundred people and I made decisions every day that affected the mission and people's lives. I would wake up every day knowing that people counted on me, were depending on me, and I did everything I could to support them and not let them down. I would work twelve- to fourteen-hour days to make this happen. I would put my life on the line for the person next to me. If something happened to them, I don't know what I would do.

I would wake up in the morning wondering why I was still alive. I wanted to let everybody know that I was there for them, just as they let me know they were there for me. We didn't worry about Washington or car payments or mortgages or nothing. We were tight, as tight as can be. We had each other's backs. We knew we could depend upon one another no matter what happened.

God, I miss that. No one here seems to understand that. They talk about Fortnight and *Game of Thrones* and Netflix. I don't have time for that shit. I want to get back and get out and do something meaningful in my life. I can't sit around and wait for something to happen; I've got to take control and make it happen. No one is going to do it for me. I have to take care of myself.

If you're going to hire me, thank you. But please have some veterans on your staff who I can relate to and talk with. Don't get me wrong, but sometimes a veteran needs to talk to another veteran, y'know? I know they try, but people who haven't served oftentimes can't understand me. I feel more comfortable with another veteran, just like you might feel uncomfortable if you worked in a place where no one spoke English. It's a connection thing, nothing more than that. Because if a veteran is not there to talk, I might feel isolated and nobody likes to be lonely when they are trying to do a good job.

7. I need a rearview mirror.

I've got to have something that puts this all behind me. You may not know this, but many of us think about going back to Afghanistan every time our head hits that pillow. I know I got this, but it's just natural because that was my life, man. My doctor gives me meds that work OK, but she also tells me that when I go to sleep, I'm on my own. My meds don't work at night. But a fifth of whiskey sure does, and I'll take that bottle anytime I can if it helps me get to sleep at night. Not waking up may be OK with me. My psychiatrist calls this nihilistic suicide.

Help me put this behind me. Pull out all the stops you can. If I fight you, please don't give up. The man or woman you loved is still there, buried behind some sand berm or some memory I can't shake. Do not give up on me, even when I give up on myself. Hide the guns and alcohol in the house but whatever you do, please do not give up on me.

8. Understand my identity.

If I felt I was different before I joined the military, I'm still different now. Like others in the LGBT community, I am working hard to find my way in a culture that is still evolving and is still trying to find full inclusion and equal rights. Support and love me without bias or unnecessary judgment. I'm not asking for anything more than love and acceptance. You don't have to understand me or my choices; you just have to accept me for who I am. I deserve the same benefits and freedoms as my straight brothers and sisters. I am a human being who is capable of love and being loved and someone who has the same basic needs as everyone else. Accept me for who I am and if you can't, please keep your mouth shut and move along. Both of us will be better off.

9. I may be more valuable to you and your company than you think.

What is your experience in hiring millennials and Gen Xers? What has been their level of experience? What are their expectations when they become part of your workforce? How long do you anticipate they will stay with your company? Are they any different from the other employees you have recently hired? Do they want to be a vice president in six months?

I've been around the world and back. Name an ethnicity and I have probably worked with someone from that background. Compare the level of responsibility your twentysomething has with what I have done in my twenties. Measure me based upon what I have done and others you may be considering. Do you understand the loyalty and character of the military today? Do you realize that I have the skill to do anything and everything that you ask of me, 24/7/365? Do you know that I have been trained to never be late, work overtime, and do whatever it takes to get the mission done?

Look past my resume, which may not have all the things you are used to seeing. Give me a chance at an interview so that you can get to know me better, and that I, too, may get to know you better.

10. I'd go back in a heartbeat.

I want to go back. My unit needs me. My job was never finished. I think about them all the time. No one understands what it's like over there. I'm doing the best I can now that I'm out, but I think about it all the time. I know I need to move on and that going back really isn't a reality for me. But a big part of me is still over there.

Things are going to get better.

Military life changed me. It may have happened at basic training when all my value systems were broken down, only to be completely rebuilt. It may have been in the field where I developed feelings with a new family. It may be a moral refocus of what I thought was important in life. I'm going to get better and I'm going to be successful. I won't let my family down and I won't let myself down.

But I still think about going back there.

EPILOGUE

What You Can Do

Life's most persistent and urgent question is, "What are you doing for others?"[1]

—Martin Luther King, Jr.

I've been searching for ways to help people and be of service for as long as I can remember. I found a lot of inspiration along the way. As early as six years of age I had already made a regular conversation connection with God, probably through the first communion teachings at Our Lady of Sorrows Catholic School. My fourth grade teacher, Sonia Gerent, was so full of love for all creatures that she grimaced when she would hear students trampling on ant hills outside. My Uncle Bert, a custodian at my elementary school, would give me unannounced gifts of grungy baseballs and mitts he would find on the school grounds—all for the joy of seeing my face when I received such treasures.

I didn't have a whole lot of friends going up, but if there was somebody different at my school, somehow I became their best friend and they became mine. I would stand alone at recess but Adam was my first best friend and the only kid of color in my first-grade Catholic school class. Chip lost a year in elementary school and he didn't know anybody in his new grade, but he became my best friend. Katie was shunned because she wore clog shoes, so we became close. Daquan was the only Chinese kid at Plant Junior High yet I became his friend and learned so much about his culture. Jafari was a lonely kid from East Africa, but boy could he throw a baseball and we spent countless hours on the ballfield at Plant Junior High playing catch.

I volunteered with a local justice system to teach math to teenage foster children. At twenty-two, I was slated to join the Peace Corps to work in a tuberculosis lab on the Ivory Coast. But I waited the weekend to get my parents' permission (which was denied) and the following Monday morning the position was gone. I'm sure many of you have your own stories of what might have been, but things still worked out for me anyway.

I've been in healthcare for over forty years. The various positions I have held—medical technologist, microbiologist, researcher, technology officer, and finally, chief information officer in managed care and hospital operations—have given me a unique perspective on the full spectrum of healthcare in the public and private sectors. I have had the privilege of meeting and working with some of the most incredible surgeons, nurses, administrative leaders, and overwhelmingly compassionate and sensitive caregivers you can imagine.

I have seen the magic of births, but also the tragedy of perfectly formed stillborn babies with an umbilical cord around their necks. I have witnessed families crying in emergency rooms and jumping for joy in surgical waiting areas. On a daily basis, patients would see me walking down the hallway believing I was a doctor that knew something about their loved ones, looking anxiously at me with hopeful eyes, yet not knowing that I was not a physician, just an IT guy.

Many people have seen the dramatic results and impact of the EN-Abled Veteran Internship and wonder how they can get involved. My usual response is, "What would you like to do?" Answers vary, but the theme remains the same.

"I want to do something that makes a difference."

"I've always thought about getting involved in something that I really believe in."

"There's got to be something more than spending two hours in my car every day."

These comments are interesting considering that they are coming from people who work in healthcare and contribute to teams that help patients every day! Still, it shows what I like to call the human condition of wanting to help people and make the world a better place.

Besides helping someone, performing good deeds makes you feel good. Helping others gives you momentary respite from your own trials and gives you new perspective and energy. By focusing on someone other than yourself, you are reminded that, as Dee Barnes stated, there are many others less fortunate than you. There is a certain calmness about being reminded what you have compared to what others can only dream of having.

Two things struck me when I returned from overseas. The first was the tastiest food I think I have ever eaten. It was a Burger King Whopper at, of all places, the Las Vegas airport. The second was walking into a very large grocery store and smiling at the food, colors, and choices I had. Silly perhaps, but I never realized how valuable simple things can be and how they can be taken for granted.

Not all of us have these experiences, but I do believe that all of us have an altruistic desire. If you've read this far, you may be wondering how you can help veterans: in your home, family, or your own community.

I have come up with a list of five ways that you can help veterans. My list is restrictive and here is why. Anyone can donate to a not-for-profit; anyone can say "thank you for your service"; anyone can put change in a cup being held by a veteran standing on a street corner. This list involves real involvement, being a contender, being involved. I'm talking real involvement, the kind that warms the soul, puts a lasting smile on someone's face, and, like Miss Gerent, lasts a lifetime.

I leave you with five things you can do to help a veteran right now.

1. Hire a veteran.

This is easy to do, but it's not easy to do right. The secret to the EN-Abled Veteran Internship was the construction, nurturing, and perpetual help given to the veteran. The EN-Abled Veteran Internship works because the culture is able to absorb, train, and advance the veteran forward like no other. To do this, fellow veterans must be involved because they can relate to veterans in ways that nonveterans can't. It's not so much a level of judgment as it is a level of sensitivity. The best way to connect people is to have people on hand that can share common experiences, and this is not just germane to veterans.

Cancer survivors can best support cancer patients. Families who have experienced the suicide of a loved one can best connect with families who have also lost a loved one through suicide. Veterans can best connect with veterans who understand what it was like to be deployed in the desert, carrying a fifty pound backpack and the realization that death can come in a moment's notice.

Integrating veterans into the workforce who can relate to new veterans coming in is the key to success, for there will be up days and down days. There will be miscommunications, often innocent, yet situations that still need explanation. The veterans will thrive in an environment that supports their strengths and improves their weaknesses. As you consider hiring a veteran, consider the effort needed and review the rewards received. The latter will provide dividends the former doesn't foresee.

Military veterans have already demonstrated leadership skills, as this is the nature of military life. This holds true regardless of the length of time in service. Young enlisted men and women are often thrust into leadership positions, whether they want them or not, whether they realize it or not. Often these leadership opportunities involve life and death decisions, a tremendous burden for someone barely out of their teens. It is rare to find such leadership schools in civilian candidates as young as in their twenties.

Military training at all levels uses age-old methods for goal setting, analysis, and performance measurement. SWOT (strengths, weaknesses, opportunities, threats) are common tools used in all branches of service and they are applied in both wartime and peace. Constant measurement and performance improvements are stressed at all ranks at all times. Military planning is always focusing on risk and performance management. It's no wonder, given the stakes that may be involved in wrong decisions or erroneous assumptions.

Given the emphasis on tasks, time, and resources, many military activities invoke project management principles in the execution of duties. That would be consistent with the emphasis on risk management and budget constraints in civilian life. Despite what most people may think, budgets are actively managed and frivolous spending is rare and far from the norm. In order to keep things in line, projects have to be managed tightly and managed well. There are consequences for those project managers whose projects fail.

You may remember a few years ago when a Soviet satellite was failing and was going to fall into the earth's atmosphere with potential catastrophic consequences. *CNN News* filed this report:

> The first opportunity for the Navy to shoot down the satellite came about 10:30 p.m. ET Wednesday. The plan included firing a missile from the USS *Lake Erie* in the Pacific Ocean west of Hawaii to destroy the satellite. "A network of land-, air-, sea- and space-based sensors confirms that the U.S. military intercepted a non-functioning National Reconnaissance Office satellite which was in its final orbits before entering the Earth's atmosphere," a Department of Defense statement said.
>
> "At approximately 10:26 p.m. EST today, a U.S. Navy AEGIS warship, the USS *Lake Erie*, fired a single modified tactical Standard Missile-3, hitting the satellite approximately 247 kilometers (133 nautical miles) over the Pacific Ocean as it traveled in space at more than 17,000 mph."[2]

While watching the news report on television, I turned to my wife, Tracy, and said, "I'll bet that the person who fired that one shot was a twenty-two-year-old kid on a ship somewhere." Sure enough, when I started asking around for more details, I found out that it was a young Navy weapons expert who fired the shot. Imagine what might have happened if he had missed?

The following quotes from veteran interns in the EN-Abled Veteran Internship highlight their commitment.

"We weren't done but everybody was packing up at 5 o'clock."

"Why can't we come in on Saturdays?"

"Why do people complain about their job? They have a job and should be grateful they have a job. There's a lot of people who don't have jobs. Why are they complaining about theirs?"

"Why are people complaining about their cars? You have a car! Isn't that good enough for you?"

I will admit, this can lead to problems. Veterans may take it upon themselves to correct these types of perceived wrong behaviors, setting up mini-cultural conflicts. The two worlds can collide and this is why it's so important to have veterans on your permanent staff. Education, not judgment, is key. Permanent staff can explain the work culture to the veteran, while at the same time, the veteran can explain the military work culture to the civilian staff. With the appropriate modification, boundaries, and understandings, teams can work cohesively on common ground.

Military personnel typically possess such team-building attributes and more. They may be experienced and self-starter leaders who are quite comfortable working on teams, following orders, performing under pressure, leading out front, and making critical on-the-spot decisions. They may also be good followers, provided clear direction is provided and lines of communication remain open. By creating a nurturing and understanding environment, such as the EN-Abled Veteran Internship, a clear understanding can be developed, fostered, and advanced.

EN-Abled Veteran Mark Truitt says it best.

"I was amazed one day when they sent me out to a clinic, by myself, to install equipment. I said, 'Who's coming with me?' 'No one,' said Tommy Bankhead, my supervisor. 'You know how to do this. Go do it.'

"I was unsure of myself, but I got the work done. When they came over to check on me later, Tommy said, 'Great job! See? I knew you could do it.'

"Then I realized, I could."

You can easily build your own EN-Abled Veteran Internship from the tools and strategies in this book. Start with just one veteran; there is no need to take on a huge burden. Learn from what this veteran has to offer and what he or she can do. See how the veteran interacts with your coworkers and customers. What you will find is a surprising and refreshing perspective from someone you thought you knew, but who gave you more than you expected.

2. Hire a veteran's family member.

Financial stress can impede physical recovery. People who worry about putting food on the table do not recover as quickly as those who do not suffer financial stress.[3] This is a unique aspect of the EN-Abled Veteran Internship method. While all of the corporate focus has been on hiring veterans, hiring a qualified and deserving family member can be equally effective.

For example, let's say a veteran is unable to work for a period of time. There may be multiple health issues, ongoing clinical appointments, a loss or drop in personal income, or a variety of reasons why a veteran is not able to work. Perhaps the veteran can no longer drive and public transportation is too expensive or out of reach.

Training and hiring the veteran family member can be an enormous godsend and something that has been totally ignored by corporate America and prohibited by law for the Veterans Administration. Yet the benefits can be the same: the development of new skills, a promising career, and a steady paycheck that the veteran family as a whole needs to keep going.

Training and hiring a veteran family member brings together and reinforces the needs and value of the cohesive family unit. Hire a veteran family member and you're helping the veteran.

3. Clinically treat a veteran.

This recommendation is for healthcare organizations. While Wounded Warriors and the Road Home Program are large and complex organizations, your own program doesn't have to be. Again, start with one healthcare provider designated to help veterans. Open it up to include families, which is something that the VA currently cannot do. Rally any veterans in your organization to provide support group opportunities. You will find a lot of veterans within your workforce if you have the courage to act.

By starting small, you can build something big. Opportunities to partner with other not-for-profits and healthcare institutions will present themselves. Opportunities for grants and other types of outside funding may occur. Before you know it, you may have a great, albeit smaller, program that can help veterans and their families. After all, isn't that what healthcare is all about?

4. Feed a veteran.

Yes, there are veterans who are homeless and go hungry. I see them on the streets of Chicago all the time. At night, they brave the elements on their own or they go to shelters. If you can support these shelters, financially or by giving them your time, you are helping a veteran.

It's always best to volunteer if you can, for that is how you get to know veterans. And they get to see you. Often just knowing somebody is there and willing to listen is something that many veterans need and it can keep up their spirits. Veterans want to be appreciated and understood, but they also want to get to know you too. Bonds develop and this is where the magic begins.

If you don't have the time, try this other strategy. Keep food and water in your car in case you run into a veteran on the street. Bring an old jacket, sweater, or blanket. Get over the notion that this blanket might be bartered for a carton of cigarettes; that's the veteran's choice and not yours. Also, make sure food is wrapped and liquids are unopened. One veteran told me he received a used water bottle spiked with antifreeze and the outcome was not good. Trust works both ways.

One of the happiest experiences I had was going home on a Friday with enough lunchtime department pizza party leftovers for the weekend. One vet came up to me and asked for a piece, and the next thing I knew two more friends followed. While I had to make other weekend food plans, I did so with a great memory and smile on my face.

5. Visit a veteran.

There are 170 VA hospitals in the United States and they are in all fifty states. Many veterans are lonely, ill, and have been forgotten. Make their day, make their week. Go visit them and bring some candy. See what happens. Share a story. Bring your family. See what happens.

You might be surprised.

APPENDIX

EN-Abled Veteran Internship Implementation Guide

TODAY'S VETERANS

Our American military is the best in the world. Extensive training, sophisticated technology, strong work ethic, and patriotism make veterans ideal candidates for the job market. Strong loyalty and devotion to service differentiates veterans from their civilian counterparts, particularly with millennials and Gen Xers. So much responsibility is given to young military members that cannot compare with any other type of occupational training.

According to the Bureau of Labor Statistics, "computer and information technology occupations [are] projected to grow 13 percent from 2016 to 2026, faster than the average for all occupations. These occupations are projected to add about 557,100 new jobs. Demand for these workers will stem from greater emphasis on cloud computing, the collection and storage of big data, and information security. The median annual wage for computer and information technology occupations was $84,580 in May 2017, which was higher than the median annual wage for all occupations of $37,690."[1]

STRENGTHS ARISING FROM MILITARY EXPERIENCE[2]

Military experience produces individuals with experiences advanced beyond their chronologic ages. With the right temperament and environment, the military veteran can be a long-term, loyal employee with a strong sense of purpose and the ability to help any organization excel. The following is a short list of skills and characters that can be an asset to any work center.

1. Leadership training: The military trains people to lead by example and accept and discharge responsibility for themselves and those who report to them. Military people "take care of their own" and bring this philosophy to the work center. Advance leadership opportunities are given to military personnel at a young age, often with other responsibilities that may include financial and project management.

2. Ability to work with multidiscipline teams and people: Essential to the military experience is the ability to work as a leader and a member of a team. Lives depend upon building these strong relationships. The military person has experience with diversity and working with all different types of people. Another example of where such experience is taught and learned at a young age.

3. Ability to work under pressure and to meet deadlines: One definite characteristic of military service is that service members must perform. They must do their job, do it right the first time, and do it in a timely manner. They are continuously setting priorities, meeting schedules, and accomplishing their missions. Pressure and stress are built into this, but service members are taught how to deal with all these factors in a positive and effective manner.

4. Planning and organization: Most military operations require thorough planning, be it strategic or operational. Military personnel planning includes careful consideration of strengths, objectives, and the management of resources, schedules, and logistics. Reassessment is ongoing. Organization, evaluation, and adjustment are continuously being assessed. The ability to participate, direct, or establish systematic planning is highly valued in business.

5. Self-discipline: In any large organization, and especially the military, there must be rules and structure to avoid chaos and internal breakdown. Individuals in the service have learned and followed rules every day in their working environment. While in this environment, they have also learned loyalty to their units and their leaders. Companies always value employees who will be "company players" and team members who follow "the rules" of the organization.

6. Character: All individuals in the service have learned to be flexible and adaptable to meet the constantly changing needs of any situation and mission. Last minute changes are not uncommon in any military or civilian working environment. Also, based on their military background, veterans are able to adapt quickly to physical and safety demands.

7. Self-direction: Many service members understand difficult and often complex issues and solve these issues or problems on the spot without step-by-step guidance from above.

8. Educated: All military soldiers have at least a GED and the majority of them have high school diplomas. Many have attended college to further their education.

9. Initiative: Many military personnel have the ability to originate a plan of action or task to answer and solve many unusual problems regarding supplies, logistics, resources, and transportation. They are able to work well in ambiguous situations.

10. Work habits: People in the military are recognized for completing their missions in a timely fashion and in an effective, efficient manner. These work habits are a definite result of social maturity, integrity, determination, and self-confidence.

THE EN-ABLED VETERAN INTERNSHIP MISSION

The EN-Abled Veteran Internship provides the necessary online and on-the-job training, resume support, and job interview skills to create a market ready professional prepared to begin a successful career in healthcare information technology.

Objectives

Recognizing the needs and value of returning military veterans, the EN-Abled Veteran Internship offers the following objectives:

- Develop skills to obtain a career in health IT with an industry standard certification in one or more applications (Epic, Microsoft, Cisco, to name a few).
- To leverage partnerships with healthcare institutions, community colleges, and our vendor community to create opportunities for veterans to learn new IT skills that make them competitive and employable in three months or less.
- Be part of a focused leading-edge electronic medical record (EMR) program. With the nationwide shortage of qualified EMR specialists, employee skills obtained through the internship will bridge the gap between military and civilian careers.

- Tell their story. Veterans will engage with employees, sharing their experiences and history and creating a greater understanding of life in the military and the sacrifices and services they made to preserve the freedoms we all enjoy.

In the healthcare information technology (HIT) field, it is common to see resumes that are full of impressive accreditations or certifications. Unfortunately, when candidates come in for interviews, they may not have operational experience or interviewing skills. The EN-Abled Veteran Internship gives such experience! Here's how:

Key component #1. EN-Abled Veteran gives the opportunity for job shadowing and skills development, giving the intern the workplace skills in a hospital environment.

The EN-Abled Veteran Internship recognizes job shadowing and skills development as a vital part to a veteran's potential for employment. Such shadowing and development should consist of the following components:

- Adequate training to give the veteran the practical information they need.
- Appropriate employee shadowing that facilitates knowledge sharing with a subject matter expert.
- Flexible scheduling to ensure time is available for the veteran to take such training.
- An engaging work center that encourages the veteran to learn and to enjoy their jobs.

Key component #2. A classroom without walls. Make available any and all current training materials that are either continuing education based or, better still, adapt entry level training already in place for new employees.

- Encourage the veteran to explore online training that may be free or readily available at low cost.
- Veterans may not have computers or high-speed internet access necessary for online training in their homes. Such tools will be necessary in order to maintain flexibility and connectivity. Consider loaner equipment and on-site access.
- Partner with organizations that are supportive of veterans. Many academic and commercial schools and businesses offer coursework

or training opportunities. Such opportunities or training may be available from prominent IT vendors.

Key component #3. Unique resume and job interviewing techniques. Provide resume refresh and mock job interview experience. Create a social media presence using LinkedIn and other social media sites. While the services can be handled by internal training teams, some consulting companies may offer similar services pro bono since they have a vested interest in veteran placement.

EN-ABLED VETERAN INTERNSHIP
TRAINING PATHWAY

In just thirteen weeks, the EN-Abled Veteran Internship seeks to match military training, military honor, discipline, and sense of service into an internship that matches the military character with an IT or HIT career. Training occurs in five stages:

Stage	Title	Length	Activities
1	Orientation	One week	Interns will review their schedule, where they will be working, and shadow the help desk and others to gain familiarity with the technology.
2	Skills development and certifications	Six weeks	Interns participate in the necessary learning and hands-on operation of working with computers and other resources to determine the needs of the intern and the potential healthcare opportunities available. Those that qualify begin the Epic certification process.
3	Resume refresh and mock job interviews	Two weeks	Prepare the interns for potential employment by providing 1:1 resume support and 1:1 mock interviews to make the student as competitive as possible in the marketplace. Meet with staffing firms for practice interviews and interview polishing. For those that qualify for Epic certification, begin projects and take the necessary examinations.

(continued)

(continued)

Stage	Title	Length	Activities
4	Job search and interviews	Four weeks	Work with staffing firms, participate in aggressive interviewing and hopefully job placement. Continue to hone skills and expand technology learning and capabilities. For Epic interns, finish examinations, achieve certification, and pursue Epic analyst opportunities. Active resume building and job interviews occur during these weeks.
5	Alumni support	Ongoing	Celebrate successes with the public and provide ongoing support for new interns and the expansion of the EN-Abled Veteran Internship.

INTERNSHIP DETAILS

Stage 1: Orientation

This stage describes the organizational components and learning environment design necessary for essential learning in both a static and mobile environment. This foundational stage establishes expectations for veterans in the internship and introduces the value they can bring to healthcare IT.

Prepare the workplace and staff for veterans.   Military service is a life experience. Veterans bring all kinds of perspectives to the workplace. They have received extensive training in many structured internships and activities. They follow orders easily and quite often possess the skills to see the big picture and to move toward a common goal. It is well understood by the veteran the importance of training, for in the military environment, failure to plan and execute at the proper time could be the difference between life and death.

Aesthetics and dynamics of the workplace should be examined to determine any gaps for incoming veterans. Included in such an analysis should be

- Physical environment
  - Is the work area ADA compliant?
  - Does the veteran have a designated workspace or cubicle to work from?
  - Are there any special accommodations that need to be addressed?

- Use of technology
  - What technology is available and how does it relate to the job task?
  - What are current policies for bringing in personal devices?
  - What software will help to do the job more efficiently?
- Other miscellaneous needs
  - Where should the veteran go for help?
  - Is there access to healthcare if needed?
  - What are the procedures for calling in sick or late?
  - Where do staff eat, socialize, mingle, etc.?

Proper engagement and support.   Veterans should be given every opportunity to achieve success, but that doesn't mean they are to be treated differently from other employees or students. The EN-Abled Veteran Internship is an opportunity and a resource, it is not a charity offering—nor do veterans want it to be. Equal opportunity means equal treatment for all.

Policies should be in place that emphasize these concepts. If veterans are to be treated fairly, they should fall under the same policies, rules, and guidelines as other employees and students. Veterans should follow the same guiding principles as everybody else. All mandatory training in the academic medical center environment should be completed by the veterans.

There are a number of military veteran agencies and the landscape is confusing. The primary source for assistance should be the Veterans Health Administration as it is a clearinghouse for helping veterans understand their benefits and the opportunities available to them.

Stage 2: Skills Development and Certifications

This stage describes the necessary learning and hands-on operation of working with computers, various IT teams, and other hospital departments. At the end of this stage, the interns would be Epic credentialed and could teach or provide support for Epic end-users. Selected veterans could also become certified in an Epic application. Credentialing is done in-house, with certification being completed by Epic.

Building the internship.   The EN-Abled Veteran Internship incorporates additional life skills and leadership principles that veterans know to expect. Given the ubiquity of healthcare information technology, those who participate in this internship have tremendous opportunities for jobs and career growth.

Assessment.   With skills and character identified, the veteran moves into the assessment phase. This phase consists of input from staff managers and directors to assess current progress and veteran potential based upon the following sample criteria.

	Outstanding	Excellent	Fair	Below Average	Unsatisfactory
Technical Skills					
Learning Acumen					
Teaching Skills					
Support Skills					
Teamwork					
Market Potential					

Stage 3: Resume Refresh and Mock Job Interviews

This stage focuses on resume development and interviewing skills. We can also begin deploying interns as add-on Epic help desk support since they will have just earned their Epic credentials.

Who better than healthcare IT professionals to work with the veteran to ensure that the right information is in a resume for a healthcare IT job? The EN-Abled Veteran Internship leverages partnerships with IT professionals and outside contracting firms that make sure the resume brings out important military experience without heavy military jargon and incorporates new skills learned through the EN-Abled Veteran Internship. The result is a polished document and a ready veteran for the next step in their career.

Relevant job interview tips include how to dress, what questions to answer, and how best to make an impression. The EN-Abled Veteran interns will have a series of practice interview sessions to better prepare them for real interviews.

Stage 4: Job Search and Interviews

This stage connects individual passions and military experiences with Epic and other IT vendor teaching and support opportunities. These interns can provide classroom, didactic, or online training to Epic end users to include new hires and refresher training. The interns will also have the opportunity to shadow directors. Veterans can start real interviews at this stage.

Since the veterans will have completed their Epic credentialing that enables them to teach Epic content, these veterans should put into practice these new skills. Such skills will help serve as resume builders for these new experiences (credentialed in an Epic application; provided go-live and on-going training and support).

With an updated resume complete, to include the hospital experience and mock job interview techniques practiced, veterans can begin to seek employment opportunities. Veterans are free to take time away from the internship to conduct interviews. Veterans who receive job offers would need to give a two-week notice, with exceptions handled by the internship director.

Stage 5: Support from the EN-Abled Veteran Alumni Association

The EN-Abled Veteran Internship is invested in our veteran interns' professional development. We keep tabs on these graduates, encouraging and helping as needed. We hope that veterans will return to periodically tell their story and encourage other veterans. For those who do come back to visit our campus, online training programs will be available to them while on the local network. They may also come back for social events, such as holiday parties, company activities, or just general fellowship. Most important, the veterans connect with those in the internship, offering guidance, encouragement, and a living example of someone who made it!

The EN-Abled Veteran Internship is unlike any other offered to military veterans today. While many companies are offering employment opportunities to transitioning veterans, the EN-Abled Veteran Internship offers a unique training approach that jump-starts careers in IT, HIT, and beyond.

If the veteran is unable to work, temporarily or permanently, a family member or significant other will be considered.

GETTING STARTED CHECKLIST

1. Identify Key Players
   - Identify a program coordinator.
   - Identify a point of contact in Human Resources for payroll, hiring, and eligibility questions.
   - Determine points of contact within your departments for job shadowing.

- Determine who will provide resume review and interview coaching.
- Determine who will provide training materials: hardware/software vendors, local colleges, veteran organizations, etc.

2. Logistics
   - Determine physical space vets will occupy and equip with necessary hardware.
   - Determine how you will host training material and provide access to vets (may be subject to agreements with training providers).
   - Determine what external and internal marketing, if any, you will provide for the program.
   - Prepare system-wide communication about the program to educate staff on program details and interacting with vets.
   - Establish a recruitment path with your local groups: VA chapter, National Able Network, Wounded Warrior, Pets for Vets, community colleges, and universities, etc.
   - Determine compensation for veteran interns.
   - Determine scope and location of recruitment.
   - Determine if and how you will assist vets with job placement.

3. Timeline
   - Finalize all key players and logistics prior to the first veteran onboarding.
   - Track progress and feedback during the first three weeks of the internship.
   - Complete an adjustment period after reviewing and discussing progress.
   - Complete regular feedback and adjustment periods.

NOTES

PROLOGUE

1. https://www.brainyquote.com/quotes/douglas_macarthur_125212, accessed December 9, 2018.

2. https://www.washingtonpost.com/national/on-leadership/wal-marts -promise-to-veterans-good-news-or-good-pr/2013/01/16/7f31da74-5fee-11e2 -9940-6fc488f3fecd_story.html?utm_term=.e0e7d2372621, accessed December 12, 2018.

3. http://www.en-abledvet.net.

4. Epic Careers, "Serve the Country in a New Way," https://careers.epic.com/ Home/Veterans, accessed October 18, 2018.

5. https://roadhomeprogram.org/our-mission/, accessed December 21, 2018.

6. https://www.dol.gov/vets/latest-numbers/ accessed January 2, 2019.

7. https://www.callofdutyendowment.org/content/dam/atvi/callofduty/code/ pdf/ZipCODE_VetReport_FINAL.pdf, accessed January 2, 2019.

8. Phil Stewart, "U.S. Military Veteran Suicides Rise, One Dies Every 65 Minutes," February 1, 2013, https://www.reuters.com/article/us-usa-veterans -suicide/u-s-military-veteran-suicides-rise-one-dies-every-65-minutes-idUS BRE9101E320130202, accessed November 11, 2017.

9. https://www.militarytimes.com/news/pentagon-congress/2018/11/21/ veterans-in-the-116th-congress-by-the-numbers/, accessed December 21, 2018.

10. https://endhomelessness.org/resource/veteran-homelessness/, accessed December 21, 2018.

CHAPTER 1: STATUS WOE

1. https://theweek.com/print/441028/85324/article, accessed January 6, 2019.

2. *The Best Years of Our Lives,* 1946 movie script, https://www.springfield springfield.co.uk/movie_script.php?movie=best-years-of-our-lives-the, accessed October 17, 2018.

3. James Jones, *WWII* (New York: Ballantine Books, 1975), 256.

4. https://www.usatoday.com/story/news/politics/2018/11/29/gi-bill -payments-va-wont-repay-vets-shortchanged-housing/2151812002/, January 2, 2019.

5. Brandon Weber, "WWI Vets Got the Short End of the Stick in the Great Depression. This Was Their Answer," December 8, 2015, http://www.upworthy .com/wwi-vets-got-the-short-end-of-the-stick-in-the-great-depression-this-was -their-answer, accessed September 3, 2017.

6. Michael D. Gambone, *The Greatest Generation Comes Home* (College Station: Texas A&M University Press, 2005), 192.

7. Ken Moffett, "Coming Home: A Study in Contrast," *Delta Winds: A Magazine of Student Essays,* 2001, https://www.deltacollege.edu/org/deltawinds/ DWOnline01/cominghome.html, accessed September 3, 2017.

8. https://constitutioncenter.org/blog/when-congress-once-used-its-powers -to-declare-war, accessed January 2, 2019.

9. CNN, "U.S. Military Personnel by Country," http://www.cnn.com/ interactive/2012/04/us/table.military.troops/, accessed December 11, 2017.

10. Greg Jaffe and Missy Ryan, "The U.S. Was Supposed to Leave Afghanistan by 2017. Now It Might Take Decades," January 16, 2016, https://www.washingtonpost .com/news/checkpoint/wp/2016/01/26/the-u-s-was-supposed-to-leave-afghanistan -by-2017-now-it-might-take-decades/, accessed September 3, 2017.

11. "The Atomic Bombings of Hiroshima and Nagasaki," Atomic Archive. com, http://www.atomicarchive.com/Docs/MED/med_chp10.shtml, accessed September 3, 2017.

12. Charles W. Hoge, *Once a Warrior, Always a Warrior* (Guilford, CT: GPP Life, 2010), xii.

13. https://www.census.gov/newsroom/facts-for-features/2017/veterans-day .html, accessed November 13, 2017.

CHAPTER 2: INVISIBLE WOUNDS

1. https://www.goodreads.com/quotes/422467-unexpressed-emotions-will -never-die-they-are-buried-alive-and, accessed December 12, 2018.

2. Notes from Trend Micro cybersecurity conference, San Antonio, Texas, May 14, 2017.

3. History.com Editors, "Psychiatrist Reports on the Phenomenon of Shell Shock," This Day in History, December 04, 1917, History.com, http://www .history.com/this-day-in-history/psychiatrist-reports-on-the-phenomenon-of-shell -shock, accessed September 3, 2017.

4. https://www.apa.org/monitor/2012/06/shell-shocked.aspx, accessed December 12, 2018.

5. Ibid.

6. https://www.apa.org/monitor/2012/06/shell-shocked.aspx, accessed December 9, 2018.

7. https://www.armytimes.com/news/pentagon-congress/2017/07/25/ptsd-disability-claims-by-vets-tripled-in-the-last-decade/, accessed December 9, 2018.

8. Stephen Joseph, "Is Shellshock the Same as PTSD?," *Psychology Today,* November 20, 2011, https://www.psychologytoday.com/blog/what-doesnt-kill-us/201111/is-shell-shock-the-same-ptsd, accessed September 3, 2017.

9. Erin P. Finley, *Fields of Combat* (Ithaca, NY: ILR Press, 2011), 158–59.

CHAPTER 3: WHEN WAR GAMES GET REAL

1. https://www.goodreads.com/quotes/8703-he-drew-a-circle-that-shut-me-out—heretic-rebel, accessed December 12, 2018.

2. John Mueller, "What's the Rush?", in Brink Lindsey and John Mueller, "Should We Invade Iraq? A *Reason* Online Debate," January 2003, https://reason.com/archives/2003/01/01/should-we-invade-iraq, accessed May 14, 2008.

CHAPTER 4: WHEN INNOCENCE
AND THE INNOCENTS DIE

1. https://www.imdb.com/title/tt0077362/quotes, accessed December 12, 2018.

CHAPTER 5: A GOLD STAR MOM'S PTSD

1. http://pzzzz.tripod.com/MomLost.html, accessed December 12, 2018.

2. See https://www.goldstarmoms.com/ for more information.

CHAPTER 6: A SENSE OF PURPOSE

1. https://www.lyrics.com/lyric/28972207/Bing+Crosby/What+Can+You+Do+With+a+General%3F+%28White+Christmas%29, accessed December 9, 2018.

2. Anna Zogas, "US Military Veterans' Difficult Transitions Back to Civilian Life and the VA's Response," University of Washington, February 2017, https://watson

.brown.edu/costsofwar/papers/2017/us-military-veterans-difficult-transitions-back
-civilian-life-and-va-s-response, accessed December 13, 2018.

3. "What Are the Biggest Challenges Facing Military Veterans?," Rally/Point
Rasmussen Reports, November 11, 2015, http://www.rasmussenreports.com/
public_content/politics/general_politics/november_2015/what_are_the_biggest
_challenges_facing_military_veterans.

4. Zogas, "US Military Veterans' Difficult Transitions Back to Civilian Life."

5. Lila Holley, CW4 (ret.), *Battle Buddy: Maneuvering the Battlefield of Transitioning from the Military* (CreateSpace, 2015), 1–2.

6. Gayle Tzemach Lemmon, "When GI Jane Comes Home," *Los Angeles Times*,
June 11, 2015, accessed September 3, 2017, http://www.latimes.com/opinion/
op-ed/la-oe-0611-lemmon-female-vets-20150611-story.html.

7. Ibid.

8. Rajiv Chandrasekaren, "A Legacy of Pride and Pain," *Washington Post*, March
29, 2014, http://www.washingtonpost.com/sf/national/2014/03/29/a-legacy-of
-pride-and-pain/?utm_term=.56b2a595e4d6, accessed June 16, 2017.

9. Erin P. Finley, *Fields of Combat* (Ithaca, NY: ILR Press, 2011), 169–70.

10. Greg Jaffe, "Criminal or Victim?," *Washington Post*, September 20, 2014,
http://www.washingtonpost.com/sf/national/2014/09/20/criminal-or-victim/
?utm_term=.0cecbbe4579c, accessed September 2, 2017.

CHAPTER 7: CAREERS, NOT JOBS

1. https://www.workitdaily.com/inspirational-career-quotes/, accessed January
5, 2019.

2. Home Base, http://homebase.org, accessed August 21, 2018.

3. For a complete list of corporations supporting the EN-Abled Veteran Internship, please go to https://www.en-abledvet.net.

CHAPTER 8: AT THE INTERSECTION
OF HUMAN SPIRIT AND THEOLOGY

1. https://www.goodreads.com/quotes/62001-we-have-just-enough-religion
-to-make-us-hate-but, accessed December 18, 2018.

CHAPTER 9: REMEMBERING
EQUALITY IN THE WORKPLACE

1. https://quotefancy.com/quote/1731411/Hilda-Solis-My-role-was-to-bring
-about-fairness-in-the-workplace-All-I-did-was-implement, accessed December
13, 2018.

2. Deborah Leuchovius, "ADA Q&A . . . The Rehabilitation Act and the ADA
Connection," PACER Center Action Information Sheets, PACER.org, 2003,
https://www.pacer.org/parent/php/PHP-c51f.pdf.

3. John R. Vaughn, "The Impact of the Americans with Disabilities Act: Assessing the Progress Toward Achieving the Goals of the Americans with Disabilities Act," July 26, 2007, https://ncd.gov/publications/2007/07262007, accessed
October 17, 2017.

4. Jimmy Lovrien, "ADA at 25: Work in Progress," *Duluth News Tribune*, July
25, 2015, http://www.duluthnewstribune.com/news/3804840-ADA-25-work
-progress, accessed January 3, 2017.

CHAPTER 10: NEW CLINICAL THERAPIES
FOR NEW TYPES OF WAR INJURIES

1. https://www.pbs.org/newshour/science/using-ecstasy-treat-ptsd-felt-like
-soul-snapped-back-place, accessed 18 December 2018.

2. Izet Masic, Milan Miokovic, and Belma Muhamedagic, "Evidence Based
Medicine—New Approaches and Challenges," *Acta Informatica Medica* 16, no. 4
(2008): 219–25, https://www.ncbi.nlm.nih.gov/pmc/articles/PMC3789163/.

3. Javier Iribarren, Paolo Prolo, Negoita Neagos, and Francesco Chiappelli,
"Post-Traumatic Stress Disorder: Evidence-Based Research for the Third Millen-
nium," *Evidence-Based Complementary and Alternative Medicine* 2, no. 4 (Dec. 2005):
503–12, https://www.ncbi.nlm.nih.gov/pmc/articles/PMC1297500/.

4. DCS (D-Cycloserine) is common in tuberculosis therapy, but the drug has
been recently used and gained acceptance in neuropsychiatric studies.

5. Judith Cukor, Megan Olden, Francis Lee, and JoAnn Difede, "Evidence-based
Treatments for PTSD, New Directions, and Special Challenges," *Annals of the New
York Academy of Sciences*, 1208, no. 1 (Oct. 2010): 82–89, doi: 10.1111/j.1749
-6632.2010.05793.x.

6. https://www.woundedwarriorproject.org/programs/warrior-care-network/
news-media, accessed January 3, 2019.

7. http://projects.huffingtonpost.com/moral-injury/healing, accessed January 3,
2019.

8. Kevin Doll post, March 9, 2017, accessed September 3, 2017, https://www
.facebook.com/RoadHomeProgram/.

CHAPTER 11: YOU CURED MY PTSD?

1. https://quotes.livejournal.com/6592114.html, accessed December 13, 2018.

2. Patrick Quinn, "Panelists: PTSD Can't Be Cured, Only Managed," Military .com, ©2018, Fayetteville (NC) *Observer*, https://www.military.com/daily-news/ 2013/04/24/panelists-ptsd-cant-be-cured-only-managed.html, accessed October 17, 2018.

CHAPTER 12: NOT YOUR FATHER'S VA

1. Joseph Shaffer can't speak but visits his local VA hospital for therapy and checkups.

2. "About VA," U.S. Department of Veterans Affairs, https://www.va.gov/ about_va/vahistory.asp, accessed September 14, 2018.

3. Leo Shane, "Vets Groups and Lawmakers Say They're Against It—But What Does 'Privatization' of Veterans Affairs Really Mean?," April 10, 2018, https:// www.militarytimes.com/veterans/2018/04/11/vets-groups-and-lawmakers-say -theyre-against-it-but-what-does-privatization-of-veterans-affairs-really-mean/, accessed September 15, 2018.

4. https://www.va.gov/about_va/vahistory.asp.

5. Pew Research Center for the People & the Press, "On Eve of Inaugura- tion, Americans Expect Nation's Deep Political Divisions to Persist," People -Press.org, January 19, 2017, http://www.people-press.org/2017/01/19/on-eve-of -inauguration-americans-expect-nations-deep-political-divisions-to-persist/#most -view-fbi-cia-doj-and-other-agencies-favorably, accessed September 15, 2018.

CHAPTER 13: MINORITY REPORT

1. See Michael D. Gambone, *The Greatest Generation Comes Home* (College Sta- tion: Texas A&M University Press, 2005), 90.

2. "Forgotten History: The Role of Women in War Times," *Chicago Tri- bune*, November 3, 2017, https://www.chicagotribune.com/suburbs/advertising/ primetime/ct-ss-pt-forgotten-history-the-role-of-women-in-war-times -20171101dto-story.html, accessed December 21, 2018.

3. National Veterans Foundation, "Transitioning from Military to Civilian: The Unique Challenges of the Female Veterans," January 24, 2017, https://nvf.org/ transitioning-female-veterans/, accessed March 27, 2019.

4. "Female Military Service (Less Ancient History," Penn State, September 23, 2016, https://sites.psu.edu/bootsandbuns/2016/09/23/female-military-service -less-ancient-history/, accessed December 10, 2018.

5. James Clark, "Here Are the Women Who First Joined Each Branch of the Military," Task & Purpose, January 21, 2016, http://taskandpurpose.com/here

-are-the-women-who-first-joined-each-branch-of-the-military/, accessed September 3, 2017.

6. https://sistersinarms.ca/history/history-women-military/, accessed December 10, 2018.

7. See Gambone, *The Greatest Generation Comes Home*, 113.

8. Shad Meshad, "Support for Women Veterans: How Long Has This Been Going On?," National Veterans Foundation, August 4, 2017, https://nvf.org/support-women-veterans-long-going/, accessed September 3, 2017.

9. Peyton Craighill, "The Wars' Toll on Female Iraq and Afghanistan Veterans," *Washington Post*, April 14, 2014, https://www.washingtonpost.com/news/post-nation/wp/2014/04/14/the-wars-toll-on-female-iraq-and-afghanistan-veterans/?noredirect=on&utm_term=.f04529855e76, accessed September 3, 2017; see also, Bianca DiJulio, Claudia Deane, Jamie Firth, Peyton Craighill, Scott Clement, and Mollyann Brodie, "After the Wars: Survey of Iraq and Afghanistan Active Duty Soldiers and Veterans," Henry J. Kaiser Family Foundation, March 29, 2014, http://www.kff.org/other/poll-finding/after-the-wars-survey-of-iraq-and-afghanistan-active-duty-soldiers-and-veterans/, accessed September 3, 2017.

10. Ibid.

11. Rosalinda Maury, Evelyn Espinoza, and James Burk, "Race Relations within the US Military," Institute for Veterans and Military Families, January 15, 2016, https://ivmf.syracuse.edu/article/race-relations-within-the-us-military/, accessed September 18, 2018. Originally published in *Annual Review of Sociology* 38 (2012): 401–22.

CHAPTER 14: THE TRANSGENDER VETERAN

1. https://seanmaloney.house.gov/media-center/press-releases/maloney-statement-on-trump-transgender-ban-in-the-military, accessed December 13, 2018.

2. Gary J. Gates and Jody L. Herman, "Transgender Military Service in the United States," The Williams Institute, May 2014, http://williamsinstitute.law.ucla.edu/wp-content/uploads/Transgender-Military-Service-May-2014.pdf, accessed September 3, 2017.

3. Jeremy T. Goldbach and Carl Andrew Castro, "Lesbian, Gay, Bisexual, and Transgender (LGBT) Service Members: Life After Don't Ask, Don't Tell," *Current Psychiatry Reports* 18, no. 6 (2016): 56, http://cir.usc.edu/wp-content/uploads/2016/04/GoldbachCastro-LGBT-Military.pdf, accessed December 13, 2018.

4. Endocrine Society, "Transgender Veterans Have High Rates of Mental Health Problems," Newswise, April 1, 2016, https://www.newswise.com/articles/transgender-veterans-have-high-rates-of-mental-health-problems, accessed January 3, 2019.

5. https://www.ywboston.org/2017/03/what-is-intersectionality-and-what-does-it-have-to-do-with-me/, accessed December 13, 2018.

CHAPTER 15: FAMILY IS A CIRCLE OF STRENGTH

1. https://www.brainyquote.com/quotes/alex_haley_391545, accessed December 13, 2018.

2. https://www.huffingtonpost.com/2011/10/27/tk_n_1035286.html.

3. Gretel C. Kovach, "Ranger from San Diego Died on 14th Tour," *San Diego Union-Tribune,* October 27, 2011, https://www.sandiegouniontribune.com/military/sdut-ranger-san-diego-died-14th-tour-2011oct27-story.html, accessed September 18, 2018.

4. https://www.huffingtonpost.com/2011/10/27/tk_n_1035286.html.

5. Elizabeth Heaney, *The Honor Was Mine* (Grand Haven, MI: Gran Harbor Press, 2016), 75.

6. Eve B. Carlson and Joseph Ruzek, "PTSD and the Family," Veterans Administration, https://www.ptsd.va.gov/professional/treat/specific/ptsd_family.asp, accessed September 3, 2017.

7. Charles W. Hoge, *Once a Warrior, Always a Warrior* (Guilford, CT: GPP Life, 2010), 256.

CHAPTER 16: BEING ALL IN

1. https://www.brainyquote.com/topics/judge, accessed December 20, 2018.

2. http://www.historynet.com/african-american-platoons-in-world-war-ii .htm, accessed December 18, 2018.

3. https://www.nationalww2museum.org/war/articles/american-indian-code -talkers, accessed December 18, 2018.

4. https://www.khanacademy.org/humanities/us-history/rise-to-world -power/us-wwii/a/american-women-and-world-war-ii, accessed December 18, 2018.

5. https://www.trumanlibrary.org/anniversaries/desegblurb.htm, accessed December 18, 2018.

6. https://williamsinstitute.law.ucla.edu/research/military-related/us-transgender -military-service/, accessed December 12, 2018.

7. https://www.historyhit.com/how-many-people-died-in-the-hiroshima -and-nagasaki-bombings/, accessed December 18, 2018.

8. https://warisboring.com/u-s-special-operations-forces-deployed-to -149-countries-in-2017/, accessed December 18, 2018.

9. https://www.thesimpledollar.com/warren-buffett-on-reputation/, accessed December 18, 2018.

10. https://www.va.gov/opa/pressrel/pressrelease.cfm?id=4074, accessed December 12, 2018.

11. Cyndy R. Snyder, Keren H. Wick, Susan M. Skillman, and Bianca K. Frogner, "Pathways for Military Veterans to Enter Healthcare Careers," Center

for Health Workforce Studies, University of Washington, May 2016, http://depts
.washington.edu/fammed/chws/wp-content/uploads/sites/5/2016/05/Pathways
_for_Military_Veterans_FR_2016_May_Snyder.pdf, accessed September 3, 2017.

12. https://www.forbes.com/sites/brucelee/2018/07/22/how-long-you-can
-talk-before-your-doctor-interrupts-you/#37d25cc14432, accessed January 4, 2019.

13. David Shulkin, "VA Improving Access to Healthcare," *The Detroit News*,
August, 27, 2017, http://www.detroitnews.com/story/opinion/2017/08/27/
shulkin-veterans-affairs-care-health-telehealth-va/105035120/, accessed September 3, 2017.

14. Justin Sloan, "Nonprofit Organizations for Veterans," Military.com, https://
www.military.com/veteran-jobs/career-advice/military-transition/nonprofit
-organization-for-veterans.html, accessed September 20, 2018.

CHAPTER 17: I, VETERAN

1. https://www.goodreads.com/quotes/834415-sometimes-people-think-they
-know-you-they-know-a-few, accessed December 9, 2018.

EPILOGUE

1. https://www.brainyquote.com/quotes/martin_luther_king_jr_137105, accessed December 8, 2018.

2. "Navy Missile Hits Dying Spy Satellite, Says Pentagon," CNN, February
21, 2008, http://www.cnn.com/2008/TECH/space/02/20/satellite.shootdown/,
accessed September 29, 2018.

3. Laura Choi, "Financial Stress and Its Physical Effects on Individuals and
Communities," December 2009, *Community Development Investment Review*, Federal
Reserve Bank of San Francisco, accessed September 29, 2018, https://www.frbsf
.org/community-development/files/choi.pdf.

APPENDIX

1. U.S. Department of Labor, Bureau of Labor Statistics, Occupational Outlook
Handbook, "Computer and Information Technology Occupations," https://www
.bls.gov/ooh/computer-and-information-technology/home.htm, accessed December 2, 2018.

2. Adapted from "21 Strengths Arising from Military Experience," National
Veterans' Training Institute, https://o6env.com/uploads/files/21%20military%20
strengths-%2006.pdf, accessed December 2, 2018.

INDEX

ADA. *See* Americans with
    Disabilities Act
Afghan National Army, 35
Afghanistan 133–134, 146; deployment
    to 35–37; life changing experiences
    and, xi, 8, 12–13, 23, 78, 128;
    transgender and, 111; VA shift
    and focus, 97; woman military
    personnel and 46, 103–104
Air Force, xiv, 17, 20, 26, 52, 96,
    104, 113
alcohol, abuse of, xi, 4, 21–22, 30,
    125, 135, 146
American Legion, 20, 113
American Psychiatric Association, 13,
American Revolution, 93, 101
Americans with Disabilities Act, 9; civil
    rights and, 67–69, 71; compliance
    with, 69–73; educating Rush staff,
    72–73. *See also* Rehabilitation Act
    of 1992
"Ashley's war," 46

Baghdad, 15, 17, 19
Barton, Clara, 101
*Battle Buddy: Maneuvering the Battlefield of
    Transitioning from the Military,* 44–45
battle fatigue, 12, 135
Beiersdorf, Marybeth, 22, 47

benefits, xi; ADA and, 68; GI
    Bill, 5, 20, 64; history of 5–6;
    inconsistencies with, 5–7, 96;
    misunderstanding of, xiv, 57;
    service connected, 29
Berlin, Irving, 41
Berlin wall, 84
"Best Year of our Lives," 3
Black Hawk Down, 25, 29
Boston Red Sox, 51
Bowie, David, 11
Brightstar, 109
British Army, 12
bronze star, 35, 46, 111, 121
Bulgaria, 7
Bunker labs, 23
Bush, George W., 19, 26, 73

Carlos, Wendy, 115
Carlson, Eve B. PhD, 124–125
Carlson, Robert D., 48–49
Campbell, D'Ann, 102
Civil War, 101
Clapp, Bobby D., 52
CNN, 152
cognitive behavior therapy (CBT).
    See new treatments for PTSD
combat operational stress reaction
    (COSR), 77

Coming Home, 25

Congress, US, xiv, xvi, 5, 7, 67, 69, 93, 96, 120, 134

Continental Army, 102

Continental Congress of 1776, 93

Cuba, 47, 126

cyberwar, 9, 134–135

Daily Show, The, 51

Department of Justice (DOJ), 85–86

Department of Veterans Affairs (VA), 64; disconnect with military service programs, 96; health Care budget, xiv, 93; health System, xiv, 20, 62; history, 93; hospitals, xiv, 5, 21, 22–23, 30. 49, 78, 85; lack of services, 20; progress with assisting veterans, 96–97; relationship with Road Home Program, 77. *See also* Veteran Rehabilitation Unit

depression, 5, 37, 84, 112, 118, 124, 128, 136; treatment of. *See* innovative treatments

Desert Storm, 5, 7, 46

Diagnostic and Statistical Manual of Mental Disorders, 13

Disabled American Veterans (DAV), 115

discrimination issues: African American and, 104–108, 131; disabled veterans and 67–73; LGBT and, 114, 116; women and, 101–107

Domeij, Kristoffer, 121–122

don't ask don't tell (DADT), 111

doughboys, 6

Drug Enforcement Agency (DEA), 86

drugs, 7; PTSD and, 78, 123; abuse and, 125; effect on families, 125

DSM. *See The Diagnostic and Statistical Manual of Mental Disorders*

Duluth News Tribune, 71

Emory Health Care, 77

EN-Abled Veterans interns: Gonzalez, Kevin, 138; Kenny, Bogumila "Bea," 83–92; Mayers, Wille, 140; Russell, Ryan, 61–64; Stein, Sid, 66, 139; Taylor, Cassandra, 104–107, 117–118; Truitt, Mark 108–100; Vasquez, Ivan and Janet, 127–129

EN-Abled Veteran internship, 23; advice for starting your own program, 58–59; history, 51–58; implementation guide, 157–166; key performance indicators, 55–56; *LinkedIn* and, 57, 109; mistakes made, 53–54; objectives, 159–160; use of staffing firms, 54, 56–57, 108, 161–162; veteran experiences. *See* EN-Abled Veterans Interns

EN-Abled Veteran support staff: Bailey, Marlene, 87; Bankhead, Tommy, 57–59, 136; Belkhos, Abdelkrim (Krim), 64–67, 90; Goings, Dwaine, 25–31, 123–124, 140

Epic Systems, xii, 53, 127–128, 137–138, 159, 161–164

Equal Opportunity Employment (EOE), 69, 10

families, xvi, 46, 53, 110, 113, 117, 150–151; family member interactions with, 122–124, 129; healing and, 37, 46–47, 51, 77–78, 80, 125–125, 140–141; importance of in PTSD treatment, xiii–xiv, 122–123, 125; outreach, 37, 116, 154; reactions to deployments, 34–35, 47–48, 126–127

Faulkner, Judy, 137–138

Federal Bureau of Investigation (FBI), 59, 85–86

Fields of Combat, 14
Finley, Erin PhD, 14, 47–48
flashbacks, xi, 77, 85, 122
Freud, Sigmund, 11

Gambone, Michael D., 56
general dysphoria, 112
Germany, 7, 15, 113, 118, 134
GI Bill. *See* benefits
Gold Star mom. *See* Road Home
    Program veteran stories
green berets, 7
Grenada, 15
Grotzke, Marissa MD, 112
Gulf War, 15

Hadfield, Chris, 11–12, 14
Haiti, 108
Harvard Medical School, 51
Harvard University 20
Hayley, Alex, 121
Heaney, Elizabeth, 127
health Information Technology (HIT)
    xii, 53, 138, 160–161, 165
Hines VA hospital, 22
Hiroshima, 8
Hoge, Charles W., 9, 127
Holley, Lila, 4445
Home Base Program, 51
Honduras, 25
House of Representatives, 8
Huffington Post, 78–79
Hungary, 7
Hussein, Saddam, 15–16, 26

Illinois Army National Guard, 47
information technology (IT), 81, 86–87,
    91, 108–110, 136, 140, 150; Careers
    for veterans, xii–xiii, 53, 88, 91,
    108–110, 140; EN-Abled Veteran
    and xii, 53, 81, 88, 150, 157–166;
    Problems with GI benefits, 5; Rush

staff and, 54; Building coalitions
    and, 54–56
innovative treatments: evidence based
    practice (EBP), 135, 137–138;
    evidence based medicine (EBM)
    75–77, 80; exposure therapy,
    76–77, 80, 135, 141; virtual reality,
    76, 80, 141
Institute for Veterans and Military
    Families, 110
International Space Station, 11
Iraq, 134; deployment to xi, 26, 42,
    128; theater operations, 7, 8, 13,
    15, 17–21, 23, 41, 47–48, 103,
    128; transgender and, 111, 118;
    transition home, 47–48, 78, 103;
    women deployment, 46, 103
invisible wounds, 9; benefits of group
    therapy, 126; comparison to similar
    injuries in WWI, 12–14; family
    effects upon 126–127; Road
    Home Program and, xiii, 37, 47,
    81; treatment. *See* Innovative
    Treatments
ISIS, 8

Jacobson, Gary, 33
James A. Lovell Federal Health Care
    Center, 86, 107–108; Veterans
    Rehabilitation Unit (VRU). *See*
    Veterans Rehabilitation Unit
Jennings, Jazz, 131
jihad, 9
Joseph, Steven, PhD, 13

Kazakhstan, 11
Korea, xi, 6–7, 133
kurds, 15, 17
Kuwait, 15

Libya, 15
Lemmon, Gayle Tzemach, 46

lesbian, gay, bisexual, transgender
veterans: coming out challenges,
113, 115, 119–120; cmployment
challenges, 117; intersection
and, 116–117; need for more
research, 111–112; transgender
troop strength, 111; unique health
challenges, 112; unique transition
challenges, 59
LGBT. *See* Lesbian, Gay, Bisexual,
Transgender veterans
Lowry, Connor. *See* Lavin, Modie

MacArthur, Douglas General, ix
Markham, Edwin, 15
mars, 12
Marshburn, Tom, 11
Marshall III, John M. 83
Massachusetts General Hospital, 51, 77
Masic, Izek,75
meals ready to eat (MRE), xi, 17
mental health and illness 9, 87,
104, 119, 124, 135; common
language and standard criteria,
13; comparison to previous wars,
12–14; family members and, 37;
transgender and, 112; women and,
103–104; *See also* alcohol, abuse
of; *See also* post-traumatic stress
disorder
Microsoft, 55
military dogs, 41
military operations in the Gulf 5, 7, 47
minority veterans, 101–107;
See Lesbian, Gay, Bisexual,
Transgender veterans and
Discrimination issues
military sexual trauma, (MST), 97,
144; incidence of, 102; Road
Home Program support, xiii, 77;
first person story of, 105–106;
severity to PTSD, 103

Moffett, Ken, 6–7
Myers, Charles MD, 12–13

Nagasaki, 8
NASA, 11
National Council on Disability,
68–69
National Veterans Foundation,
101–102
New Jersey Medical School, 51
Niger, 7
North County Independent Living
in Superior (northwestern
Wisconsin, 71

Once a warrior, always a warrior,
9, 127

Panama, 15, 25
Parent, Tracy ix
Patrick Sean (D) New York, 111
Pearl Harbor, 6
Pete (GI): PTSD and, ix; transitioning
home and 41–43
Pew research center, 94
Post-Traumatic Stress Disorder
(PTSD), xiii; contradictions, 9;
invisible wounds and. *See* Invisible
wounds law enforcement issues
and, 29–30, 48–49; medication
management and, 59, 72; non-
combat and, 8; Road Home
Program and. *See* Innovative
treatments and Road Home
Program staff stigmas and.
See Stigmas

Rasmussen reports, 43
Rehabilitation act of 1973, 67–68
Republican guard, 15, 26
Revolutionary war, 93
Richards, Renee, 115

Rigg, John, MD, 7
Road Home Program veteran stories:
    Beiersdorf, Will, 47, 125–127;
    Friese, Tanya, 112–114, 123, 132;
    Lavin, Modie, 33–37; Miller, Chris,
    16–24, 78, 123, 140; Williams,
    Tanjilisa 104, 131
Road Home Program treatment
    team: Brennan, Michael MD,
    43–44, 79, 125–126; Karnik,
    Niranjan, MD, PhD, 80–81,
    135–136; Pollack, Mark, MD,
    51–52, 54, 58, 80, 125
Romanenko, Roman 11
Romania, 7
Rush Medical College, 51
Rush University Medical Center:
    EN-Abled Veteran. *See* EN-Abled
    Veteran. *See* Road Home Program
Ruzek, Joseph PhD, 124–125
Ryan, Paul, 120

Sales, Leila, 143
Salt Lake City Veterans Affairs Medical
    Center, 112
Salute, Inc, 22
sense of purpose 23, 31, 41–49, 109,
    123, 127, 129, 136, 145, 157
Shaffer, Valerie and Joseph, 93
shellshock, 12–13, 75
Shinseki, Eric K., 47
silver stars, 46
Simon, Ken, xii
Soldiers project, 114
Solis, Hilda, 67
Somalia, 15, 108
Soviet Union, 15
Starbucks, 84–85, 91
State of the American Veteran, xi
Stewart, Jon, 51
stigmas: PTSD and 48, 63; hiring prior
    military, 63; asking for help, 79;

female veteran and, 106; African
    Americans and 107; family members
    and, 124; transgender and, 132
Suicide, 66; rate, xiv, 135–136;
    homelessness and, 5; bombers and,
    8, 48, 133, 145; mental illness and
    112, 118, 146; family and 140, 151
surgical strikes, 9
Swift, Jonathan, 61

thousand mile stare, 12
Tran, Lac, 52
traumatic brain injury, (TBI), xiii, 12,
    62, 77, 97, 116, 125, 145
Trend Micro, 11
Tressler, Gaelynn Lea, 71
Truman, Harry S, 131

US Department of Veterans Affairs
    National Center for PTSD, 124
USAjobs.gov, 91

VA Medical Center Philadelphia, 38
Veterans Evidence-Based Research
    Dissemination and Implementation
    Center, 14
Veterans Rehabilitation Unit, 63,
    94–96, 107–108; Dee Barnes and,
    45–46, 150
Viet Nam, xi, 5, 15, 52, 93; Congress
    and, xvi; different scope of benefits
    and, 6; transition home, xi, 6; type
    of war, 7, 15, 20, 133
Voight, Jon, 25

Walmart, xii
Weber, Brandon, 5
Weekend at Bernie's, 22
Weyand, Frederick C.,
    General, 6–7
What can you do with a General, 41
What doesn't kill us, 13

Williams, Monnica, 75

Wood, David, 78–79

World War I: psychiatry and, 12–13, 75; transition home and, 5; women and, 101

World War II, xi, xvi, 3, 13, 101–102, 122; lack of diversity, 131; comparison to today's wars, 7, 133–134; greatest generation and, xi, 122; transition home, 4–7

Wounded Warrior Network xiii, 20, 77, 154, 166

Yeomans, Peter 78

Zogas, Anna, 43–44